History 13-16 Project

CW00969477

China

Paul Davies

Education Officer for Dorset LEA and formerly
Head of History, Harry Carlton School, Nottinghamshire

General Editor: Ian Dawson, Trinity and All Saints' College,
Leeds

Published under the aegis of the School Curriculum Development Committee by

Holmes McDougall,   Edinburgh   1988

Acknowledgements

The author and the publisher acknowledge the following illustration sources. They have made every effort to trace the copyright holders but where they have failed, they will be happy to make the necessary arrangements at the first opportunity.

We are grateful to the following for permission to reproduce illustrations:

Auckland Collection   78 (top)
Barnaby's Picture Library   52
BBC Hulton Picture Library   6 (middle right), 8, 10 (bottom right), 16 (bottom), 19 (bottom), 20 (top), 21 (left and right), 23, 29 (bottom), 32 (left), 33 (bottom), 39 (top), 41 (top left), 45, 47, 49, 60 (right), 61 (top and bottom right), 62, 63
Kevin Callagher   33 (top), 83
Camera Press   8 (top right), 15 (right), 28 (bottom), 30 (bottom), 58, 68 (bottom)
China Now   30 (top)
China Pictorial   22 (left), 26
China Reconstructs   87 (top), 88 (top right, left and bottom)
Chris Cullen   6 (middle), 75 (top)
Mary Evans   42 (bottom)
Foreign Language Press   10 (left), 11 (top and bottom), 28 (top)
Les Gibbard   79 (bottom right)
Swan Hellenic   36
Sally and Richard Greenhill   9 (top)
Hong Kong Government Office   8 (top right)
Hutchison Library   5 (top left)
London Zoo   5 (middle right)
Mansell Collection   10 (top), 14 (middle right), 15 (top left and bottom left), 17 (bottom right), 18, 19 (bottom), 41 (top right and bottom), 43 (top), 44
Musee Royal de l'Armee et d'Histoire Militaire   77 (top)
Photo Source   29 (top), 91
Popperfoto   17 (bottom left), 26 (middle), 65, 72
Punch   93
Radio Times   34 (top)
Scotland-China Association   67
Snark International   42
Telegraph Newspapers   77 (middle)
Travel Photo International   5 (bottom left)
Society for Anglo-Chinese Understanding   5 (top right), 5 (middle left), 6 (top and middle left), 6 (foot), 9 (bottom left and right), 26 (left), 32 (right), 33 (foot), 36 (top), 48, 54 (bottom), 60 (left), 68 (top), 69 (bottom), 85 (top, middle and bottom), 87 (middle left, middle right and foot)
United Nations   77 (bottom)
Xinhua News Agency   51

For Andrea

Further information on the History (13-16) Project can be obtained from The Information Centre, School Curriculum Development Committee, Newcombe House, 45 Notting Hill Gate, London W11 3JB: The Director, Schools History Project (13-16), Trinity and All Saints College, Brownberrie Lane, Leeds LS18 5HD

Illustrations by Denby Designs and David Wilson

Cover picture by permission of Travel Photo International

Holmes McDougall Ltd, Allander House, 137-141 Leith Walk, Edinburgh EH6 8NS

ISBN 0 7157 2618-8

© SCDC Publications 1988. All rights reserved. No part of this publication may be reproduced, stored in a retrieval system, or transmitted, in any form or by any means, electronic, mechanical, photocopying, recording, or otherwise, without the prior permission of the copyright holder.

Printed and bound in Great Britain by Holmes McDougall, Edinburgh

Contents

Understanding your world

Here is the news

Every day there is news — news in the papers, news on the radio, news on the television. You're probably more interested in some news items than others: for instance, you may be interested in a news item because it affects *your* area — what's happening in schools, or employment chances in your town. However, many news items aren't about your town or even your country. They're about other countries — places you haven't been to, places you may never go to. Why should you be interested in news from far away places? Why might the news in these headlines be important to *you?*

Understanding the news

These headlines include things you hear about again and again — terrorism, famine, wars, worries about what other countries or people will do. The news tells us what's happening today, but we often need to look elsewhere to understand people's ideas and actions — why they are frightened of other countries, and why they attack their enemies.

Some of the reasons lie in the past. Studying the past can help us understand the present — understand today's headlines. This book investigates China's past. This will help you understand better why China is like it is today; why China is friendly with some countries but not others and how China may develop in coming years. Before we begin this modern world study we need to know something about the Chinese people. Do they have the same ideas and customs as British people? Is their way of life the same? How is China different? What do the illustrations on pages 5-9 tell you about China today?

China — a different world

START HERE

5	4	3	2	1
好 謝 謝 再 見	我 很 好 您 呢	您 好	我 是 中 國 人	我 是 英 國 人
HAO XIE XIE ZAI JIAN	WO HEN HAO NIN NE?	NIN HAO?	WO SHI ZHONG GUO REN	WO SHI YING GUO REN
WELL THANKS THANKS. AGAIN SEE	I VERY WELL. YOU TOO?	YOU WELL?	I AM CHINESE NATION PERSON	I AM ENGLISH NATION PERSON
Very well thanks; see you again.	I am very well. How are you?	Are you well?	I am Chinese.	I am English.

China — a land with a history

China in the world

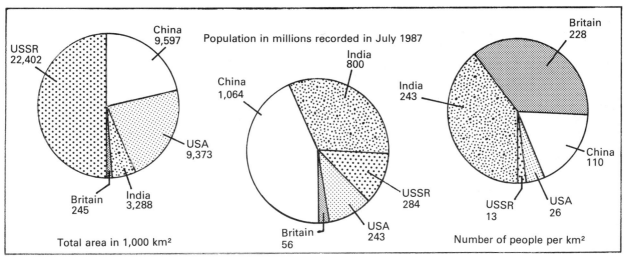

Population in millions recorded in July 1987

USSR 22,402 · China 9,597 · USA 9,373 · India 3,288 · Britain 245

Total area in 1,000 km²

China 1,064 · India 800 · USSR 284 · USA 243 · Britain 56

Britain 228 · India 243 · China 110 · USA 26 · USSR 13

Number of people per km²

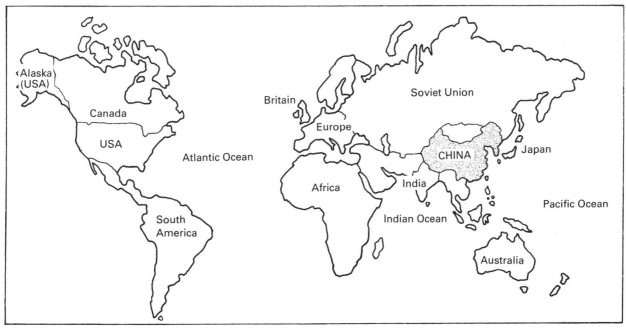

Alaska (USA) · Canada · USA · Atlantic Ocean · South America · Britain · Europe · Africa · Soviet Union · CHINA · Japan · India · Indian Ocean · Pacific Ocean · Australia

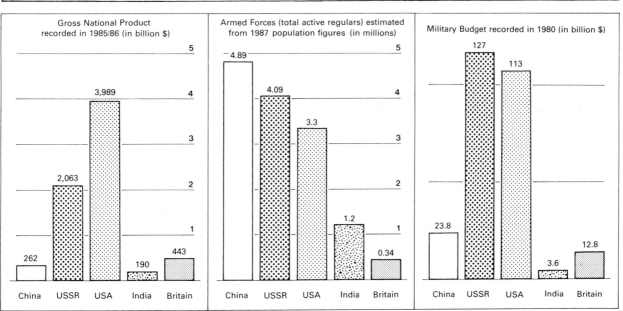

Gross National Product recorded in 1985/86 (in billion $)

China 262 · USSR 2,063 · USA 3,989 · India 190 · Britain 443

Armed Forces (total active regulars) estimated from 1987 population figures (in millions)

China 4.89 · USSR 4.09 · USA 3.3 · India 1.2 · Britain 0.34

Military Budget recorded in 1980 (in billion $)

China 23.8 · USSR 127 · USA 113 · India 3.6 · Britain 12.8

Sources: Jane's Almanac of World Military Power 1980 and The World Factbook 1987 (C.I.A.)

Inside China Today

Sally and Richard Greenhill

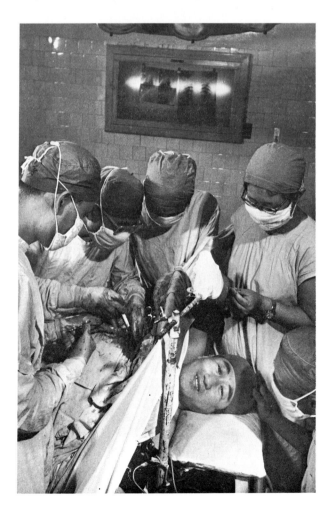

Understanding China today

A world of differences

As you have seen, China is very different from Britain in size, in its history, in its customs and in the way of life of the people. You couldn't go to China and just settle easily and quickly into school. Too many things would be different and difficult to understand.

China is different from Britain. But China is also very different from China a hundred years ago. There have been many changes in China during the twentieth century, as the life story of one man, Pu Yi, shows.

1908 — Pu Yi, aged three, at the time of his accession to the Dragon Throne.

1917 — Pu Yi at the time of his brief restoration to the Throne. He had been deposed in 1911.

1932 — Pu Yi at the time of being made Emperor of Manchukuo by the Japanese. This was the third occasion he held the title of Emperor.

1945 — Pu Yi at the trial for war criminals held after the end of the Second World War.

1971 — Pu Yi working as a gardener in the former imperial palace.

China — a Modern World Study

Pu Yi — the emperor who became a gardener. Why did this man's life change so much? We can only answer that question by looking at the history of China in this century. Studying China will also help you understand more about the world today and the news headlines you see. The history of China also reflects important twentieth-century ideas and changes such as Empire, Communism and Capitalism. We can also learn how these changes have affected the lives of ordinary Chinese people as well as altering China's relations with other countries.

Studying China should also help you to understand about the lives of people very different from yourself. China, like many other countries this century, has tried to change quickly to cope with the inventions, wealth and ideas of Europe and the USA. At the same time these 'Third World' countries want to keep their own traditions and values. In other words, how can countries balance the 'best of the old' and the 'best of the new'?

To sum up, in studying the story of China this century we can understand:

- important concepts such as Empire, Communism and Capitalism
- how and why change takes place
- how different people live, and how they react to events and changes in their countries
- how a country's past can influence what is happening today
- how countries react to changes in other countries.

And, perhaps the most important reason for studying China this century is that it is a fascinating story of a remarkable people. A people who today make up one quarter of the world's population. The French Emperor Napoleon said 'Let China sleep. When she wakes the world will be sorry'. China needs to be understood, and to do that China's history needs to be studied.

China, Britain and the West

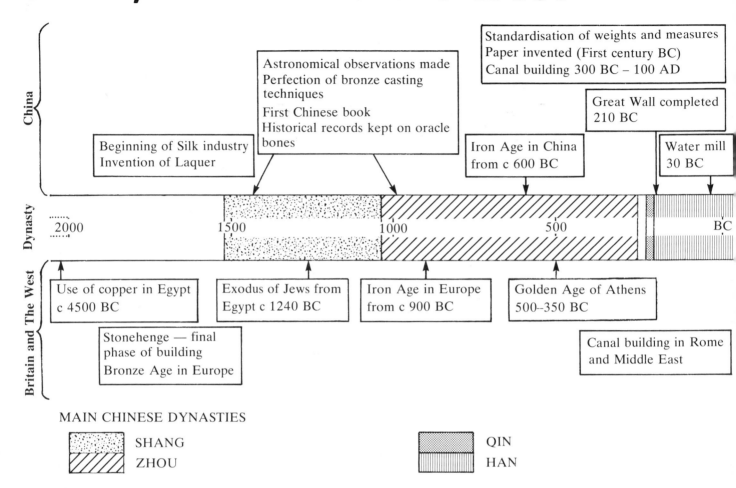

China

Astronomical observations made
Perfection of bronze casting techniques
First Chinese book
Historical records kept on oracle bones

Standardisation of weights and measures
Paper invented (First century BC)
Canal building 300 BC – 100 AD

Great Wall completed 210 BC

Beginning of Silk industry
Invention of Laquer

Iron Age in China from c 600 BC

Water mill 30 BC

Dynasty

2000   1500   1000   500   BC

Britain and The West

Use of copper in Egypt c 4500 BC

Exodus of Jews from Egypt c 1240 BC

Iron Age in Europe from c 900 BC

Golden Age of Athens 500-350 BC

Stonehenge — final phase of building
Bronze Age in Europe

Canal building in Rome and Middle East

MAIN CHINESE DYNASTIES

SHANG
ZHOU

QIN
HAN

China in the 20th Century

Significant turning points

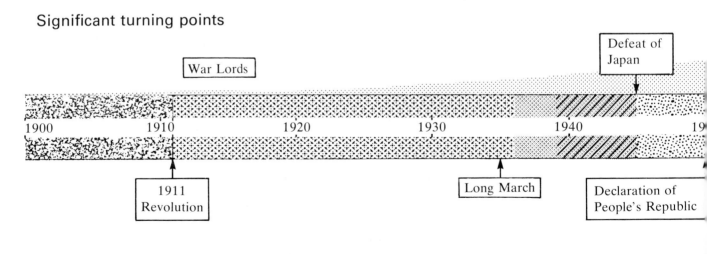

War Lords

Defeat of Japan

1900   1910   1920   1930   1940   19

1911 Revolution

Long March

Declaration of People's Republic

Rule of Last Emperors
Nationalist Rule

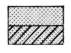
Japanese Invasion
World War II

Period of growth/development in China

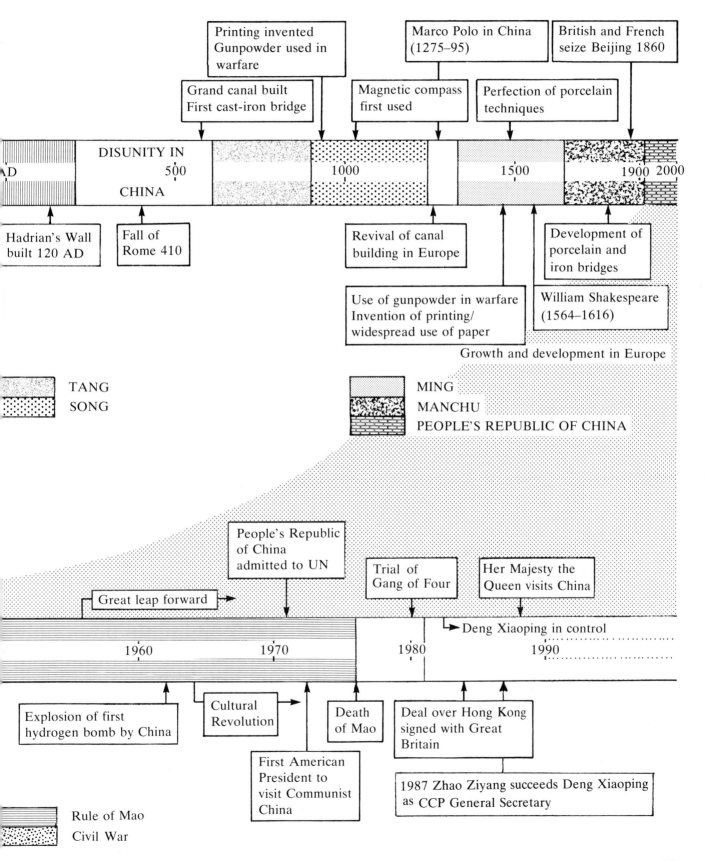

Printing invented
Gunpowder used in warfare

Marco Polo in China
(1275–95)

British and French
seize Beijing 1860

Grand canal built
First cast-iron bridge

Magnetic compass
first used

Perfection of porcelain
techniques

DISUNITY IN
500
CHINA

1000

1500

1900 2000

Hadrian's Wall
built 120 AD

Fall of
Rome 410

Revival of canal
building in Europe

Development of
porcelain and
iron bridges

Use of gunpowder in warfare
Invention of printing/
widespread use of paper

William Shakespeare
(1564–1616)

Growth and development in Europe

TANG
SONG

MING
MANCHU
PEOPLE'S REPUBLIC OF CHINA

People's Republic
of China
admitted to UN

Trial of
Gang of Four

Her Majesty the
Queen visits China

Great leap forward

Deng Xiaoping in control

1960

1970

1980

1990

Explosion of first
hydrogen bomb by China

Cultural
Revolution

Death
of Mao

Deal over Hong Kong
signed with Great
Britain

First American
President to
visit Communist
China

1987 Zhao Ziyang succeeds Deng Xiaoping
as CCP General Secretary

Rule of Mao
Civil War

The Power of the Emperors

'Our Court of Heaven'

China has the longest continuous history of any nation in the world. China's civilisation stretches back for nearly 4000 years; it developed an advanced way of life and a highly organised society long before Europe. Sources 1, 2 and 3 show how this affected the attitudes of Chinese rulers to other countries and peoples.

SOURCE 1

A fifteenth century Chinese illustration of a westerner. What do the Chinese seem to think of westerners?

SOURCE 2

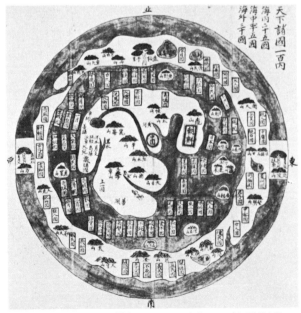

A nineteenth century Chinese map of the world. "Middle Kingdom" is the dark side of the disc in the centre. What does this suggest about Chinese attitudes to other countries?

Paper making.

The use of gunpowder.

SOURCE 3 — A message from the Emperor

Though you, O King, live far beyond the sea, you have respectfully sent to Us a mission. Your envoy has crossed many seas and paid his respects to us at the Celestial Court. You beg for one of your people to stay at our Court of Heaven. This cannot be; it is not our Custom. The distinction between Chinese and barbarians is more strict. We need nothing from you. We have all things. We do not value strange or ingenious objects. The manufactures of your country are not of the slightest use to us. We have commanded your tribute-envoys to return home. It is your duty, King, to obey Our wishes. Everlasting Obedience to the Dragon throne of China will bring peace and riches to your land. We send as presents to you valuable silks and elaborate curios — all precious things. Note the kindness with which We treat you.

(a letter sent by Emperor Qian Long to King George III of Britain in 1793)

China's supremacy

Why did the Chinese Emperors believe they were superior to all other people? Part of the answer can be found by comparing Chinese developments with those in other countries, part by looking at the power of the Emperors inside China.

14

China's achievements

Long before Europeans the Chinese had an understanding of astronomy and mathematics. They put their ideas to practical use, as these pictures show.

▶ *Look back to the time-chart on pp. 12–13. When were these skills developed in China and the West.*

Use of the magnetic compass.

Porcelain production.

Kow-towing before the Emperor. The custom of kneeling and knocking head on the ground was expected of all who came before the Dragon Throne, even foreign ambassadors.

The Emperors in China

Within China, the Emperor did not share power with anyone. In theory he was in total control, although he was isolated from the millions of people he ruled. He was called the 'Son of Heaven' and, from his dragon throne, he issued commands or 'decrees of heaven' for everyone to obey. He was fabulously rich and lived in splendid luxury pampered by hundreds of servants.

▶ *This power and wealth could be used for great construction projects and memorials – how do they demonstrate the power of the Emperors?*

The model army of Xian. The Emperor Qin Shihuangdi had a vast tomb built for himself and his army at Xian. Instead of burying his army, as was the custom, each soldier was sculpted in terra cotta together with his horses and his chariots and the models were buried in the tomb. It is said that the Emperor then ordered the thousands of peasants who had worked on the tomb to be buried alive.

Change under the Emperors?

If China and its Emperors were so strong, why was there a revolution in 1911? After all, life in China had not changed greatly over many hundreds of years. The Emperors themselves saw no need for change. Why change a system which made you great and all-powerful?

The size of China

Although its size varied over the centuries (depending upon whether or not the Emperor was winning wars) China was always an enormous country. In the eighteenth century travel in China was no harder than in Europe, but a routine order from Beijing took 56 days to reach Guangzhou in the far south. Even the fastest express messenger took 32 days (at an average speed of 63 miles a day!). An ordinary message to Chengdu in the west took 48 days, an express messenger 24.

▶ *How would the great size of China affect the way the country was governed?*
▶ *Would it encourage changes in government?*

Local Government

The Emperor's orders were carried out by local officials called mandarins. Some mandarins had very great power, governing as many as 250,000 people. They were responsible for keeping law and order — torture, and execution of criminals by beheading, were common. They also collected taxes, and

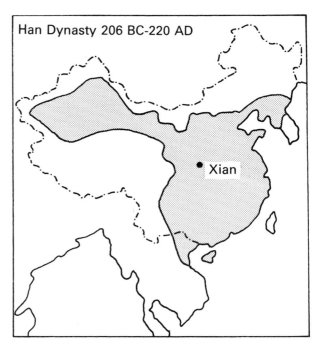

The extent of the Chinese Empire at the time of the Han Dynasty.

dishonest mandarins could make a lot of money by cheating the peasants.

▶ *Other factors also contributed to the lack of change in China. On these two pages you can see some of them. How do they each help to explain the lack of change in China?*
▶ *Would mandarins, such as the one shown here with his family, be anxious for change?*

The extent of the Chinese Empire at the time of the Qing Dynasty.

The people

Over 80% of the people were poor peasants. Life was very hard as they tried to grow enough rice or millet to eat on their tiny plots of land (usually 0.2 hectares — about 0.5 acres). Rapid population growth (from about 100 million people in 1750 to over 400 million at the end of the nineteenth century) caused further hardship as good land became scarcer. There were many examples of families being so poor that children were sold to raise money for food. In these circumstances the peasants could own very few possessions. There was also little chance of educating children to improve conditions.

Industry and trade

There was little industry in the China of the Emperors: most people worked on the land. However some industries did develop in the towns, mostly producing luxury goods such as silk, furniture and porcelain (called 'China' in England). These goods became very fashionable in Europe and there was a great demand for them. However, the Emperors did not want to trade with European merchants and tried to keep these 'foreign devils' (as they were called) out of their 'celestial empire'.

The family and customs

The family was the centre of Chinese people's lives. Following the teaching of Kong fu-zi (Confucius), the father was master in his house and women were treated as inferior. Men expected unquestioning obedience. Even the wives of mandarins were expected to occupy themselves with reading, embroidery or playing chess. Chinese women followed the tradition of binding their daughters' feet from the age of five to make them small and dainty. Marriages were arranged for young people by their fathers, although the young people themselves had probably never met. The bride's father would be compensated with money for the loss of his daughter. The family included the living and the dead. Religious ceremonies were held to honour the memory of dead ancestors, and each family thought it essential to have a son to continue these ceremonies.

A peasant farmer. Would he be able to change his way of life?

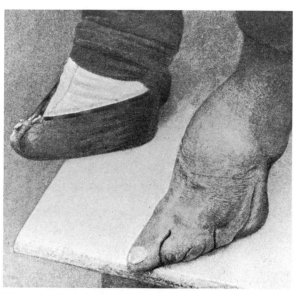

The deformed feet of a Chinese woman who had them bound when she was seven years old. When she grew up walking would be almost impossible. What does this tell us about the power of customs?

17

The beginnings of revolution

Although there had been little change in the government of China this didn't mean that everyone was happy with it. Some of the features that hampered change also created anger and resentment. The living conditions of the peasants, for instance, had caused rebellion in the past, but the Emperors had always regained control.

'An invasion of wild beasts'

In the nineteenth century a new factor was stirring up trouble — the interference of foreign countries in China. During the nineteenth century Britain, France, Germany and others began to trade with China. Britain traded in opium. British merchants carried opium from India to sell in China, filled their ships with Chinese products such as tea and silk, and sold them back in Britain. This trade was very profitable, and few people asked whether it was right to trade opium.

A Chinese cartoon from c. 1910 titled "The foreign beasts are attacked". Why did these feelings also build up hatred against the Emperor of China?

When the Chinese authorities tried to stop the opium trade, the British and French sent gunboats to bombard their ports. The Chinese quickly lost what is known as 'The Opium War'. They were forced to sign treaties allowing Europeans to run Chinese ports. Foreign consuls ran the port areas, foreign police forces patrolled them and Europeans organised customs duties. (All this in a country which was not theirs!)

SOURCE 4 — The opium trade

Money is leaving the country in large quantities, being drained by the opium trade. This trade is the work of the English. They have come to China, and brought us a disease which will dry up our bones and bring ruin to our families. Since the Empire first existed it has had no such danger. It is worse than an invasion of wild beasts. I insist that the smuggling of opium be punishable by death.

(a Chinese official, 1838)

18

Foreign countries competing to carve up China. How would Chinese people have felt about this?

The 1911 Revolution

By the beginning of the twentieth century there were many people in China who criticised the rule of the emperors. They complained about centuries-old problems like poverty. Many were also ashamed at the way China had been taken over by foreign powers. They blamed China's weakness on its system of government, and plotted to overthrow the emperors.

The main group of rebels was the Chinese Revolutionary Alliance, led by Sun Yat-sen. Their chance came when the Dowager Empress Ci Xi died in November 1908 and was replaced by a 3-year-old boy called Pu Yi. When the rebellion came, in 1911, there was no one to uphold the power of the Emperor — and the rebellion became a revolution. But who were to be the new rulers?

Not only were European powers gaining influence in China but China's army was defeated by the people they called the "eastern monkeys" — the Japanese. This picture shows the surrender of a Chinese general to the Japanese in 1895.

19

Who will rule China?

Chaos

The rebels who began the revolution wanted Sun Yat-sen to be the new leader. In fact the first President of the new Republic of China was Yuan Shi-kai. Yuan was powerful because he was the army commander. Sun at first did not oppose him for fear of risking more civil war.

Although he was powerful, Yuan could not control the whole of China. All over the country local leaders set up their own governments, backed by their own private armies. These local 'warlords' terrorised their own areas for their own profit. Yuan and the army generals in Beijing — and Sun Yat-sen, who finally set up his own government in Guangzho — could not control them.

Japanese invaders

More problems came from outside. Japan took advantage of China's weakness and invaded China. In 1915 Japan presented the 'Twenty-one Demands'. These gave Japan great control over the Chinese people, especially in the north.

SOURCE 5 — Extracts from the Twenty-one Demands

ARTICLE I.   The Chinese central government shall employ influential Japanese as advisers in political, financial, and military affairs.

ARTICLE IV.   China shall purchase from Japan a fixed amount of munitions of war (say 50 per cent or more of what is needed by the Chinese government) or that there shall be established in China a Sino-Japanese jointly controlled arsenal. Japanese technical experts are to be employed and Japanese material to be purchased.

(quoted in Charles Meyer and Ian Allen, 'Source Materials in Chinese History', 1970)

The effects of the revolution

The revolutionaries of 1911 had complained about the poverty of the people, the cruelty of local government and the interference of foreign countries. None of these problems had been solved. Why had there been so little progress?

Yuan Shih-Kai, the general who tried to make himself an Emperor. Was he likely to be successful?

Rivals for government

Out of the chaos came two groups who hoped to end China's troubles — the Guomindang (GMD) led by Sun Yat-sen, and the Chinese Communist Party. At first the two groups were able to work together. Both had been influenced by the success of the revolution in Russia in 1917, although Sun did not think that Communism was the right answer for China.

The aims of the two groups are shown below:

▶ *How different are their ideas?*
▶ *Do you think the two groups could work together?*
▶ *Which people would these ideas appeal to?*

GMD Aims

1 China should become a prosperous and developed country.

2 China should be free from foreign interference.

3 China should be strong enough to compete with European countries such as Britain and France.

4 Eventually, the people of China should become better off and be given more freedom.

CCP Aims

1 The state should take land from the landowners and redistribute it among the peasants.

2 The state should own and organise industry so that profits should not go to the rich factory owners but should be used to benefit everyone.

3 The people should be made more equal.

4 The people should have more say in running their own lives and governing the country.

5 All these things should happen as soon as possible after the CCP came to power.

Chiang Kai-shek, leader of the GMD. Chiang's success in building up the GMD army was based on his experiences in Japan and Russia. His power as army commander made him Sun's successor.

The body of Sun Yat-sen is carried to its burial. Why was Sun so important in keeping the GMD and CCP together?

The struggle for power

At first co-operation worked. Many CCP members joined the GMD army and fought to defeat the warlords and resist the threat from Japan. However, Sun died in 1925. The new GMD leader was Chiang Kai-shek, and he turned against the communists. He believed he needed the support of foreign merchants, factory owners and bankers to make China strong and prosperous again. These were the very people the communists wanted to destroy in a workers' revolution. Chiang therefore decided to begin a campaign of terror against the communists. Thousands of communists were rounded up in the major towns and executed.

21

The defeat of Chiang Kai-shek

The attack on the communists

Led by Chiang Kai-shek, the GMD took control over most of China. Only the CCP was standing in Chiang's way. Chiang was so powerful that the CCP was forced to retreat. The CCP's main base was established in a remote southern area called Jiangxi. Even then Chiang and the GMD were determined to destroy them and 'extermination campaigns' were launched to finish off the CCP. The CCP seemed to have little chance, but they survived and gradually turned the tables. In 1949 they took control of China. How did they do this?

The Long March

In Jiangxi the CCP built up a strong force known as the Red Army. This army fought off Chiang's attacks, but in 1934 Chiang tried a new tactic. He decided to starve out the CCP. The CCP's answer was to break out of its Jiangxi base and head for a safer area to the west. Thus began what the communists called the 'Long March'. They did not know it at the time, but their search for a remote, safe base would take them 6000 miles away and would take a year to complete.

After many dangers — they were pursued all the way by the GMD and crossed mountains, swamps and rivers — the CCP arrived in the town of Yanan in Shaanxi Province. Only 10% of the army reached the safety of Shaanxi. As they travelled through western China they freed many areas from warlord rule and gave the peasants the land. A strong leader also emerged — Mao Zedong.

▶ *How might this event help to explain the eventual defeat of the GMD?*

Red Army soldiers crossing the grassland swamps on the Long March.

The Japanese war

While the GMD and CCP were fighting each other the Japanese invaded from the north. They first seized the northern province of Manchuria and then pressed south. The CCP, now in the north, tried to halt this advance using guerrilla tactics, and encouraged the GMD to join them to resist this foreign invasion.

At first Chiang refused and sent some troops up to Shaanxi. He believed his first priority was to destroy the communists and not to weaken his forces by fighting the Japanese, but his troops in the north refused to obey him. In a bizarre incident, Chiang flew to the north only to be kidnapped and imprisoned by his own officers. They refused to release him until he agreed that the GMD troops should fight alongside the Red Army to defeat the Japanese invaders. Thus began another period of co-operation when the GMD and the CCP fought together against a common threat to China.

▶ *How might these events explain the final defeat of the GMD?*

The Japanese occupation of China.

KEY

▨ The Japanese Empire 1930   ▥ Occupied 1933-35

▥ Manchuria, annexed 1931-32 ▧ Occupied 1937-45
renamed Manchukuo

◉ Chongqing from 1937 the capital of Nationalist China

Japanese troops in northern China. How would the Chinese people respond to the GMD and CCP attitudes to Japanese attacks?

The defeat of the Japanese

Eventually the Chinese struggle against the Japanese invaders became part of World War II. China found herself a new ally, the United States of America, which was also at war with Japan. The USA sent help to China, to the government of Chiang Kai-shek. However, Chiang was still reluctant to make an all-out effort to fight the Japanese. He continued to believe the CCP was his real enemy and conserved his strength for the expected struggle with the CCP. Chiang said the Japanese were 'a disease of the skin' whereas the CCP was 'a disease of the heart'. In contrast the Red Army, using guerrilla tactics, fought well against the Japanese. The Red Army made a point of treating the peasants well, and quickly won their support. The area they controlled in northern China was now growing.

The Chinese weren't strong enough to defeat Japan by themselves, but did enough to help weaken Japan. When Japan surrendered to the USA in 1945 (after the dropping of atomic bombs on Hiroshima and Nagasaki) she also withdrew her army from China.

Civil War in China

By 1945 China had suffered nine years of war against Japan. There were several attempts to bring the CCP and the GMD together to sort out the chaotic state of the country. But neither side trusted the other and a full-scale civil war began. The GMD had about 3 million men under arms, supported by American supplies, against the CCP's one million. The GMD expected a quick victory, yet within three years it had suffered a total defeat. Entire GMD armies surrendered to the communists without a fight. In January 1949 Beijing surrendered, and in October Guangzhou fell to the CCP. The Civil War was over, and Mao Zedong proclaimed the new People's Republic of China. The GMD and Chiang Kai-shek fled to the island of Taiwan.

▶ *Why were they defeated?*
▶ *Had any of China's problems been solved during this period of civil war?*

23

Communism — the answer to China's problems?

Karl Marx's theory

The founder of modern communism was Karl Marx, a German writer and thinker who lived in Britain from 1850 to 1883. He worked out a completely new theory of how things change in history and how countries should be organised. Communist countries like Russia and China have used his ideas in different ways but they all accept his main argument.
Quotations from Karl Marx's works.

THE WORKERS HAVE NOTHING TO LOSE BUT THEIR CHAINS. THEY HAVE A WORLD TO GAIN

FROM EACH ACCORDING TO HIS ABILITIES, TO EACH ACCORDING TO HIS NEEDS

WORKERS OF THE WORLD UNITE!

CAPITALIST

control

control

Means of production

Transport

Land

Factories

profits

wages

work

History and the revolution

Marx said that in history there had always been one 'ruling class' which ran the government and kept the other classes down. But sooner or later one of these other classes would become strong enough to overthrow the ruling class and seize power itself. Marx argued that 'revolutions' like this were certain to happen. They would happen first in industrial societies, though it was hard to be sure exactly when the revolution would come.

The class struggle

Marx said that in Britain and other leading countries the factories, the land, the railways, the mines, and all the other 'means of production' were owned by 'capitalists'. The capitalists also controlled the government, and used the army and the police to keep the workers in their place. The workers owned nothing, had no control over their work and gained none of the profit. So there was a 'class struggle' between capitalists and workers.

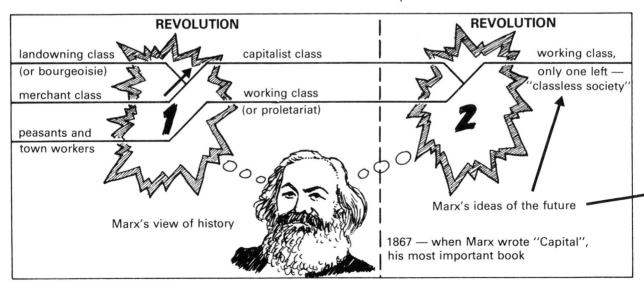

REVOLUTION

REVOLUTION

landowning class (or bourgeoisie)

capitalist class

working class, only one left — "classless society"

merchant class

working class (or proletariat)

1

peasants and town workers

2

Marx's ideas of the future

Marx's view of history

1867 — when Marx wrote "Capital", his most important book

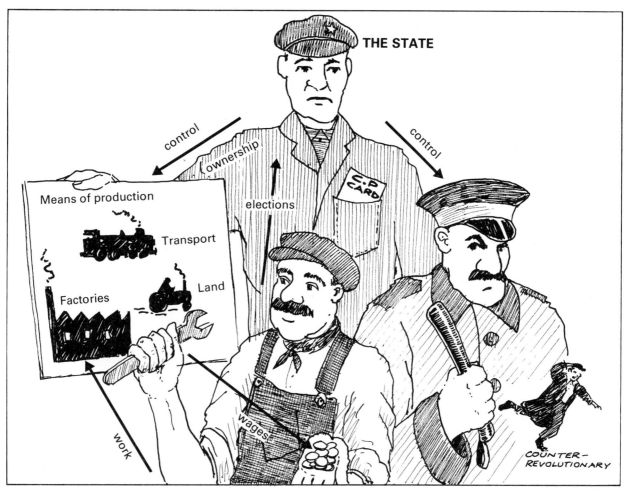

What happened?

In 1917 in Russia, and in 1949 in China, Communist Parties following the ideas of Marx seized control of their countries and took over control of the means of production — they carried out successful revolutions. The Communist Parties claim to represent the working class. They set up strong state governments to put down the enemies of the revolution, and to organise the changeover to communism.

When communism was fully established there would be only one class, so there could be no more class conflict. A strong state would not be needed any more.

Workers of the world unite!

Marx set up an international movement. 'Workers of the World Unite,' he wrote in 1848, 'You have nothing to lose but your chains.' He argued that wars were started by capitalists to divide the working class and to make profits out of armaments. Communists hoped that once the revolution started in one country it would spread quickly to the whole world. But they expected the capitalists in the other countries to fight hard to stop this, and to stamp out the revolution.

▶ *What classes of Chinese people would be likely to accept Marx's ideas?*
▶ *What class would dislike them?*
▶ *How would you expect communism to deal with China's problems?*
▶ *Marx's theory claimed that the revolution was certain to come in the end. How would this help the communists?*
▶ *What differences can you see between the communism predicted by Marx and the communist states established in this century?*

25

Communism and the people

Victory brings many problems

▶ *The chart below shows the problems Mao faced.*
He promised great changes. Did they happen?

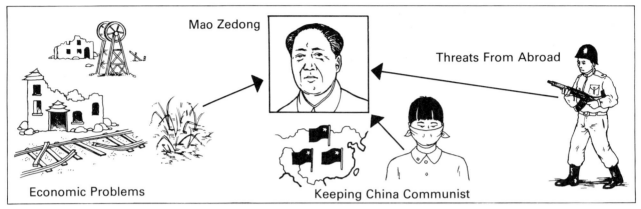

Economic Problems

Mao Zedong

Threats From Abroad

Keeping China Communist

On 1st October 1949, from the top of the Gate of Heavenly Peace in Beijing, Mao Zedong, Zhou Enlai and other communist leaders watched a great procession of Red Army soldiers, peasant fighters and other party workers go past in a triumphal march. Mao had just announced the foundation of the People's Republic of China. This 'liberation' was the victory for which Communists had fought for over a quarter of a century, and so it was a day of great rejoicing.

However, after such a long period of fighting and chaos China needed to be rebuilt. Factories had been destroyed, railway lines ripped up and farms ruined. Worse, the old problems that had caused the 1911 Revolution had still not been solved. Mao told his fellow communists:

> 'We still have much work to do. The remnants of the enemy have yet to be wiped out. The serious task of economic construction lies before us.'

Mao proclaims the People's Republic of China in 1949. Would Communism bring the answers to China's problems?

Who owns the land?

For centuries the poverty of so many Chinese people had caused resentment and rebellion. One of Mao's decisions was to see that the landlords in the countryside were removed and their land redistributed to the peasants. Landlords were brought before People's Courts and tried for crimes against the peasants. They were nearly always found guilty immediately, and in one year over 2 million landlords were executed.

A People's court.

Mao then hoped to give the land to the peasants as a reward for their support of the Red Army, but he soon realised that their small plots were uneconomic. In 1955 he began a policy of encouraging small farms to join together into co-operatives so that peasants could work together to make their land more productive. In two years 800,000 co-operative farms were set up. The peasants were organised into production brigades along military lines. Huge construction schemes were begun to build terraced fields and irrigation ditches. The work was done by thousands of peasant workers.

Industrial targets

At the same time industry was being built up. The damage to factories caused by the wars was repaired, but new heavy industry schemes were needed. A five-year plan was organised so that production of coal, steel, electricity and petrol could be increased. Targets were set for each industry and the people were made to work harder. By 1957 these targets had been exceeded, but it was realised that further progress would require even greater sacrifices from the Chinese people.

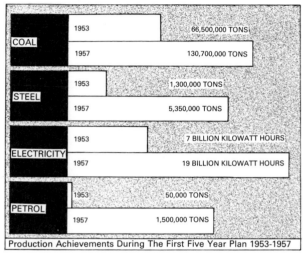

COAL		
1953	66,500,000 TONS	
1957	130,700,000 TONS	
STEEL		
1953	1,300,000 TONS	
1957	5,350,000 TONS	
ELECTRICITY		
1953	7 BILLION KILOWATT HOURS	
1957	19 BILLION KILOWATT HOURS	
PETROL		
1953	50,000 TONS	
1957	1,500,000 TONS	

Production Achievements During The First Five Year Plan 1953-1957

The Great Leap Forward

In 1957 Mao launched this new campaign to develop China with the slogan 'Work hard for three years, be happy for a thousand.' This success would require a 'Great Leap Forward'. He realised that the entire country needed to be organised to produce more. Co-operative farms were reorganised as communes which might contain as many as 100,000 people. The commune was responsible for industry, agriculture, education, welfare and defence. The peasants lived and worked as equals, and as well as the mass production of food they were encouraged to assist industry by setting up 'backyard furnaces' to produce iron. Large construction projects, such as the building of the Sinani River Hydroelectric Power Station, were also carried out.

The Great Leap made people realise the importance of hard work and co-operative effort, but it couldn't achieve all its targets. Such rapid change was very difficult and was also very dependent on Russian aid. When the Russians withdrew their technicians and financial aid because of political disagreements the problems grew. Two years of bad weather followed, leading to bad harvests and famine.

▶ *In what ways do the peasants' lives seem to have changed?*
▶ *Was life in China changing for the ordinary people?*
▶ *Can we assume all Chinese saw an improvement in their lifestyle, such as described in Source 6?*

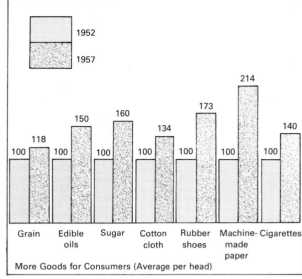

More Goods for Consumers (Average per head)

Grain 100/118, Edible oils 100/150, Sugar 100/160, Cotton cloth 100/134, Rubber shoes 100/173, Machine-made paper 100/214, Cigarettes 100/140

1952 / 1957

SOURCE 6 — Changing lifestyles

Pong Xiujing, an old resident, describes the changes that she has seen in her lifetime.

'Our lane has changed.

I'm seventy years old this year and have been living in Nanyutai Lane for 33 years. What great changes I've seen!

Before liberation, our lane had three "manys" — many poor people, many slum houses and many children. People made their lives by selling their labour—pedalling pedicabs, doing odd jobs, running small stalls. None of them had a fixed job. Many families did not know where their next meal would come from. The houses they lived in were in a terrible state, with the wind whistling through the cracks in the winter and the rain leaking through the roof in the summer. But in those days who cared about us?

With liberation in 1949, we working people stood up and became masters of the new society. As soon as the People's Liberation Army men entered the city, they provided us with food, money and clothes. They got us together and explained the revolution to us. The people's government began solving the problems of unemployment and we all got steady jobs. Some went into factories and others joined producers' co-ops. With stable monthly wages, our life improved steadily.

Our people's government thinks of everything for us. More than 100 families in our lane have moved into new apartments or houses. The homes of the others have been well repaired. The street's housing management office always asks for the opinion of the neighbourhood representatives before they distribute or renovate housing. If anything goes wrong with the electricity, water or drains, we just tell the office and it sends repairmen right away.'

(from 'China Reconstructs', August 1973)

Keeping China communist

Winning control

When Mao's rule began in 1949 he was concerned to keep China communist and stamp out any remaining opposition. He was especially determined not to allow foreigners to regain control of China. Cadres, or bands of communist party workers, were sent out into the countryside to teach the people about communism and root out any opponents. Propaganda for the Communist Party was used everywhere to persuade people of the correctness of communism and the wisdom of Chairman Mao. And, of course, the economic organisation of the country meant that Chinese people were controlled. The communes and co-operatives regulated people's lives.

▶ *Was Mao able to keep control and prevent criticism of his communist government?*
▶ *He had promised great changes, but would everyone agree that the right things were being done?*

Education or control?

Mao also introduced a crash programme to teach reading and writing. Before 1949 most of the peasant population of China was illiterate, but by 1958 only 20% of the population under 45 years old could not read or write. Now most of the population could at least read instruction manuals and propaganda posters.

The 100 Flowers Campaign

Opponents of the new communist government under Mao were severely dealt with. They were sent away to 're-education camps' where, after some punitive persuasion, they nearly always became communist supporters.

Commune members studying quotations from Chairman Mao during a break from work. Is this good evidence of support for Mao?

A change came in 1956. Mao called for anyone with ideas about how China should be run to speak out. He used symbolic words: 'To the artists and writers we say: Let a hundred flowers blossom, let a hundred schools of thought compete.' There was a barrage of criticism of communism, and then Mao called a halt. He said that there were 'poisonous weeds' among the 'fragrant blossoms'. It has been said that Mao was not interested in hearing the ideas of non-communists but was out to identify his opponents so that he could silence them permanently.

Part of a revolutionary exhibition in Canton. The models show a wicked landowner on his knees, being forced to read the thoughts of Mao. Why was this kind of scene put in an exhibition?

The Cultural Revolution

After the failure of the Great Leap Forward Mao's position became insecure. His policies did not seem to be working, and the '100 Flowers Campaign' showed there were many critics. For a time Mao resigned as Chairman of the People's Republic of China. Mao had argued for more collective work, for large construction schemes, and for the running and planning of factories to be led by the workers rather than by experts. This last point caused a split in the Chinese Communist Party. Some leaders believed China should model itself on the Soviet Union and allow the creation of a privileged class of scientists, engineers, managers and technicians. This would stimulate industrial growth such as there had been in the Soviet Union. Mao totally disagreed with the creation of an elite group of this kind. He said it was anti-communist and should be smashed. However, it was not until 1966 that his reputation had recovered sufficiently for him to do something about it.

Propaganda posters in Beijing. Why was education important for successful propaganda?

The Red Guards

An unusual event put Mao firmly back in the public eye. On 25 July 1966 Mao, at the age of 72, swam nine miles down the fast-flowing river Changjiang in sixty-five minutes. This event, which was surrounded by a blaze of publicity, seemed to appeal to the youth of China and in particular a group of young extremists called the Red Guards.

Mao wanted to use this group to launch his campaign to regain control of the leadership of China and to root out any 'bourgeois thinking'. He wanted to destroy the elite group of managers and party officials and create a purely communist society where everyone was equal. Millions of young people, mainly schoolchildren and university students, joined the Red Guards. Mao told them they had a 'right to rebel' against anyone in authority who did not have pure communist views.

Mao published a collection of his ideas called 'The Thoughts of Chairman Mao' and this Little Red Book, as it became known, was adopted as the bible of the Red Guards and freely distributed throughout China. In the late summer of 1966 the Red Guards moved into action. They forbade shopkeepers and hairdressers to sell Western-style clothes or to give Western-style haircuts. The sale of alcoholic drinks, perfume, cosmetics and antiques was also banned. In bookshops, fiction was replaced by collections of Mao Zedong's writings. Flower shops and a stamp shop in Beijing were closed on the grounds that stamp collecting and having flowers in the house were bourgeois customs.

Taxis, private cars and first-class railway travel were condemned, and passengers on pedicabs were ordered to pedal themselves while the driver sat in the passenger's seat. There were even demands that traffic lights should show red for 'go' and green for 'stop'. In all this chaos there were an untold number of acts of brutality, and many thousands were killed. No criticism of Mao's ideas and policies was tolerated.

Mao swimming in the Changjiang at the age of 73. Why did this swim gain so much publicity?

The effects of the Cultural Revolution

By 1969 the violence and upheaval of the Cultural Revolution was at an end. Mao and his prime minister, Zhou Enlai, emerged as the two most powerful men in China. Lin Biao and others who had opposed Mao in the early 1960s fell into disgrace, and in 1971, after a supposed plot against Mao, Lin fled to the USSR. En route his plane crashed in the wastelands of Mongolia, killing everyone on board.

In the early 1970s Mao's thoughts were put into practice. Schools taught the thoughts of Mao Zedong and children learned the importance of serving other people. Children were also taught the value of manual work and school time was set aside for construction projects.

Children in Yanan helping to build foundations for an extension to their school. Why were all Chinese children expected to do manual work like this?

"Little Red Soldiers" on parade. Why was Mao especially keen to win the support of the young?

Communes were made the centre of 85% of Chinese people's lives. By 1975 about 75,000 communes existed, and in each one the importance of the people's role in governing the commune's affairs was stressed. Managers and other privileged groups were not allowed. Urban communes were set up in the towns, and these organised all aspects of people's lives from nursery schools for working mothers to street cleaning, and from organising squads of part-time soldiers to social work. Prices and wages became controlled by the government. All young people had to serve for two years in the People's Liberation Army. Even Mao's wishes for complete equality seemed to have been realised: everyone now wore the Mao boiler suit, which was available in three standard sizes. Mao was in a supreme position of power, worshipped as a hero by millions of Chinese people.

► *Were these the kinds of changes promised by Communism?*
► *Did they solve the problems that had plagued China for centuries?*
► *Can you see any link between this style of government and the teachings of Kong Fu-zi and the rule of the Emperors?*

China and the Superpowers

Allies or enemies?

In 1949 Mao's communist government was new but not secure. The GMD forces in Taiwan threatened to re-invade the mainland and topple the government. Mao feared that the USA would help the GMD because the USA feared the spread of communism to other countries in Asia.

Who would be China's ally? The USSR was powerful and communist. China and the USSR seemed natural allies, and China and the USA natural enemies.

A changing situation

The many conflicts near China and the changing policies of the three countries meant that China's relationships with the USA and the USSR changed. The chart below shows what happened.

▶ *Has China been able to follow an independent foreign policy?*

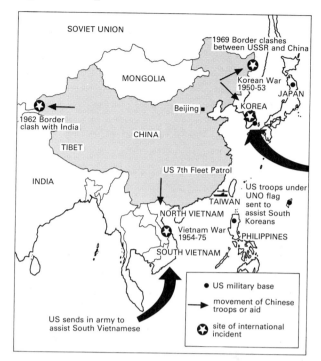

▶ *The map above shows the range of conflicts near China's borders while Mao was ruler. Would these conflicts confirm or undermine China's attitudes to the USSR and the USA?*

A Summary Chart of China's relations with the Superpowers.

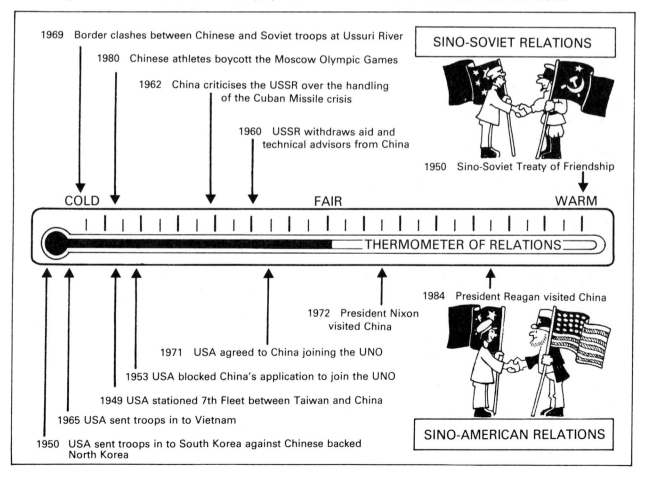

31

Politics after Mao

The problem

SOURCE 7 — What will follow Mao?

Loyal parents who sacrificed so much for the nation
Never feared the ultimate fate.
Now that the country has become Red, who will be
  its guardians?
Our mission, unfinished, may take a thousand years.
The struggle tires us and our hair is grey.
You and I, old friend, can we just watch our efforts
  being washed away?

(a poem written by Mao to his fellow-leader, Zhou Enlai, 1975)

In this poem, Mao is raising the problem of what will happen when he is dead. It is exactly the same problem that the Emperors had faced in previous centuries — how can you be sure that the next rulers will keep to your policies?

By 1976 Mao had ruled China for 27 years and organised the Communist Party for 41 years, but now he was old and in poor health. Yet he had made no plans for a successor. A struggle for power began during the last months of Mao's life. Who would win — and would new rulers change Mao's policies?

The contestants

Two groups of politicians wanted to rule China. They had very different ideas about how China should develop, as you can see below.

▶ *Do their differences remind you of past arguments about how to improve life in China?*

The Radicals
Leaders: The 'Gang of Four', led by Jiang Qing (Mao's wife).
Policies: They opposed the moderate policies. They thought the moderates were moving away from communism and Mao's thoughts. They wanted to return to the ideas of the Cultural Revolution — to abolish all private businesses, to make Chinese people more equal and to reduce foreign influence. Their support came mainly from the young.

The Moderates
Leaders: Zhou Enlai (d. 1976), Deng Xiaoping.
Policies: They won influence in the early 1970s while Mao was still alive. They wanted to modernise China and thought that China needed Western help. Therefore China's trade with the West increased — even European fashions were seen in China.

Jiang Qing, Madame Mao.

Deng Xiaoping.

The struggle for power

When Zhou died in January 1976 the group of left-wing radicals began to exert more influence in China. Mao was old and very weak, and in the final months of his life he was unable to resist the pressure of this group. Led by Mao's wife, Jiang Qing, they persuaded the dying Mao to remove Deng Xiaoping from all his posts. He was publicly ridiculed. His enemies picked on his height — he was under 1.5m (5ft) tall. They said 'How can you trust a man who has to wear his trousers up under his shoulder blades?'.

A cartoon published in "The Observer" in September 1985. What does this tell us about Deng's policies?

More than 50,000 people filed past the body of Mao Zedong at the lying-in-state. His body has been preserved in a huge mausoleum in the Square of Heavenly Peace. Great care was taken to set up his tomb exactly in the north-south direction because this line was sacred to the Emperors. Would Mao have approved of this?

When Mao died in September 1976 the left-wing radicals tried to seize power. However, too many powerful people were opposed to them. The Gang of Four were arrested in October 1976. They were charged with plotting to seize power and with personal responsibility for killing 34 000 people in the years of the Cultural Revolution. The following year posters appeared on walls in the capital demanding the return of Deng. His nickname was 'little bottle' and people hung red bottles of ink from trees to show their support for him. Deng was reinstated to all his old positions, and by 1980 felt sufficiently secure to put the Gang of Four on trial. The trial was televised, and the Chinese saw the wife of their former leader and hero in the dock. Jiang Qing was defiant to the end. She shouted at the judges 'You are trying to destroy me because you know you can never destroy Chairman Mao.' She was sentenced to death, but her sentence was changed to life imprisonment in January 1983.

This series of events clearly shows how by the early 1980s Deng was determined to remove the strictness of Maoist communism and to begin what he called the 'Great Leap Outwards'.

Madam Mao being taken from the courtroom after she was sentenced to death. This created a problem for Deng. Should he order her execution or reduce the sentence to life imprisonment? In the end Deng reduced her sentence. Why might he have done this?

Helping the people?

Too many people?

The most important consideration in discussing China's economy is the size of its population. In 1983, the census showed that for the first time there were over 1 billion people in China. This vast population causes all kinds of problems for its leaders apart from those of growing and importing sufficient food.

For example, about 6 million Chinese (the equivalent of the population of Switzerland) die each year. This creates surprising difficulties — burying 6 million people would in theory require 4 000 hectares (10 000 acres) of land and more then 2 million cu. m. (70 million cu ft) of timber! The government is trying to encourage more cremations as at the moment only 30% of the dead are cremated. The government has also launched a fierce campaign to slow down the growth rate of the population, and strict laws have been passed to limit each couple to only one child. Even if this 'One Child Policy' works it is estimated that there will be an extra 200 million Chinese by the end of this century.

Moving away from communism?

Deng Xiaoping, who remained General Secretary of the Chinese Communist Party until October 1987, was prepared to move China away from Mao's strictly communist policies. He was often quoted as saying 'it does not matter what colour the cat is as long as it catches mice'. He was prepared to allow some private ownership of land, some private selling of farm produce and he opened up trade with the West in order to move China forward.

The policy of the Four Modernisations was launched by Deng. Its aim is to update China's industry agriculture, defence and science and technology in order that China is transformed into an economically advanced country by the year 2000. China now seeks technical assistance from more technically advanced countries such as the USA, Japan, West Germany and Britain. The new leadership, headed by Zhao Ziyang seems likely to continue this policy.

► *Compare this attitude with that of the emperors as stated in Source 3, page 14.*

SOURCE 8

A cartoon published in the ''Radio Times'' in June 1980. Does this tell us any more about the nature of Deng's policies?

SOURCE 9 — Deng Xiaoping's speech

'China will remain socialist while marching towards a new prosperity . . . The basic things will continue to be state owned . . . but we must open up China to the outside world if we are to achieve our aim of quadrupling output and turning China into a world economic power by the twenty-first century.

'I think some old comrades fear that after they fought all their lives for socialism, for communism, suddenly capitalism is coming back. They can't bear it, they are afraid. Your fears are baseless. Our open door policy is harmless as we can deal with any bad capitalist influences. We must not close our doors again, as we did in the 1950s; if we did we would not be able to catch up with developed countries in the next 50 years.'

(speech to the Central Advisory Commission, 22 October 1984, as reported in 'The Times', 2 January 1985)

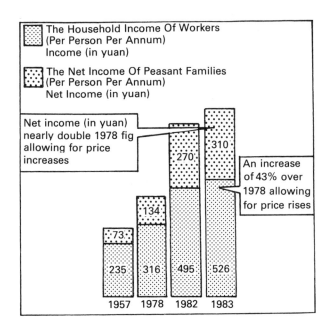

The Household Income Of Workers (Per Person Per Annum) Income (in yuan)

The Net Income Of Peasant Families (Per Person Per Annum) Net Income (in yuan)

Net income (in yuan) nearly double 1978 fig allowing for price increases

An increase of 43% over 1978 allowing for price rises

	1957	1978	1982	1983
Income		134	270	310
	73			
Net Income	235	316	495	526

SOURCE 10

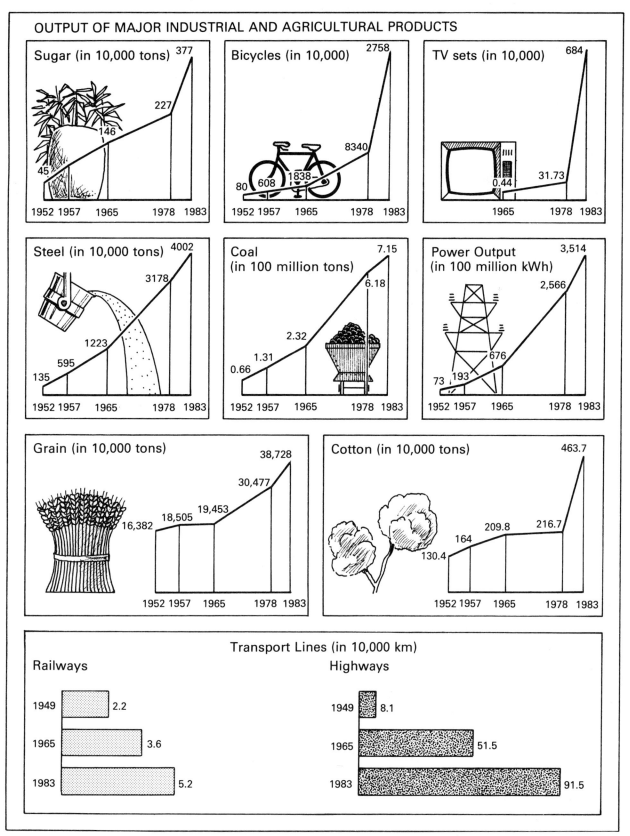

OUTPUT OF MAJOR INDUSTRIAL AND AGRICULTURAL PRODUCTS

Sugar (in 10,000 tons) — 377, 227, 146, 45 — 1952 1957 1965 1978 1983

Bicycles (in 10,000) — 2758, 8340, 80, 608, 1838 — 1952 1957 1965 1978 1983

TV sets (in 10,000) — 684, 0.44, 31.73 — 1965 1978 1983

Steel (in 10,000 tons) — 4002, 3178, 1223, 595, 135 — 1952 1957 1965 1978 1983

Coal (in 100 million tons) — 7.15, 6.18, 2.32, 1.31, 0.66 — 1952 1957 1965 1978 1983

Power Output (in 100 million kWh) — 3,514, 2,566, 676, 73, 193 — 1952 1957 1965 1978 1983

Grain (in 10,000 tons) — 38,728, 30,477, 19,453, 18,505, 16,382 — 1952 1957 1965 1978 1983

Cotton (in 10,000 tons) — 463.7, 209.8, 216.7, 164, 130.4 — 1952 1957 1965 1978 1983

Transport Lines (in 10,000 km)

Railways
1949 — 2.2
1965 — 3.6
1983 — 5.2

Highways
1949 — 8.1
1965 — 51.5
1983 — 91.5

▶ *During the Cultural Revolution period (1966–70) production figures were not issued. Is it fair to assume that the production at that time increased steadily as these graphs show?*

▶ *All these figures are issued by Government agencies in Beijing. To what extent can they be trusted?*

▶ *Do these statistics show that China's problems have been solved?*

Finding out about China

A new China?

The Four Modernisations and more contact with the West have had two major consequences in China. Firstly, China has become much more influenced by the West. This has affected all aspects of life from religion to eating habits. Secondly, and perhaps even more startling, is the news that Mao is no longer being treated as a god. He is being criticized, and it is even being claimed that he made some mistakes.

It sounds as if China has changed a great deal, but has it? Our information is largely obtained through Western news reports, like those on these pages. Do they tell us what China is really like? For example, most Chinese people's social habits are perhaps much the same as they were 10, 50, or even 200 hundred years ago.

During the Cultural Revolution all religions were suppressed in China. Everyone was encouraged to worship Mao. Now religious worship is permitted although closely regulated. Here Chinese Muslims listen to a sermon in Harbin, northeast China. Why would the Chinese government be pleased to see such pictures in the western press?

CHINA 'TO CHOP CHOP- STICKS'

By HUGH DAVIES
in Hongkong

CHINA'S one billion inhabitants have been urged to stop using chopsticks in favour of the more hygienic knife and fork.

Hu Yaobang, Communist party chief, told a group of peasants in Peking: "We should prepare more knives and forks, buy more plates and sit around the table to eat. Chinese food in the Western style — that is, each from his own plate.

"By doing so, we can avoid contagious diseases."

Hu recently entertained a group of foreign correspondents at his home to a French meal. The table was laid with knives and forks; wine was served in crystal goblets.

More civilised

Backing for his remarkable statement came yesterday from the PEOPLE'S DAILY, China's official voice, which said that the Western style of eating reflected a "civilised, healthy and scientific way of life."

It added that there was a real danger of passing on disease by the traditional method of eating from a common dish with chopsticks.

Endemic Chinese diseases, such as hepatitis, could be greatly reduced if plates, knives and forks were used, the paper stressed.

Hu has also called on Chinese to beef up their daily diet by consuming milk, meat and other high proteins instead of rice, wheat and vegetables.

"That would be a great victory, one of great importance for a fundamental turn for the better in the constitution of the Chinese people," Hu said.

A Chinese visitor to Britain saw this extract and commented that this was news in the west but would be ignored by the Chinese. Would this kind of change be likely to take place? Why would a British newspaper want to report on this "change"?
(Daily Telegraph 21/12/84)

Philately no longer a crime in China

By GRAHAM EARNSHAW in Peking

STAMP collecting has suddenly become a big fad in China after more than a decade of being banned as a bourgeois, decadent hobby.

The stamp bug has attacked with such vengeance in the past year that it is hard to squeeze into some post offices because of the crowds of collectors outside swapping and selling stamps to each other.

Collection destroyed

For some people, the crowds of philatelists bring back painful memories.

"I used to collect stamps," said an older man standing on the outskirts of the crowd outside one post office. "But my whole collection was seized and burned by the Red Guards during the Cultural Revolution. I could never start collecting again."

Millions of stamps must have been burned in the late 1960s by the Maoists. Houses were ransacked, stamp shops closed, and their contents destroyed.

Nowadays, Cultural Revolution stamps are the most popular, especially those featuring the late Defence Minister Lin Piao, who was hailed as Chairman Mao's successor until he reportedly tried to murder his mentor in 1971.

Lin Piao stamps can sell for £3 or £4 or more each on the streets — about a week's wage for most Peking workers.

But probably the most highly-sought modern Chinese stamp is one put on sale for only a few hours one day in 1969, called "The whole of China is Red" with the Chinese mainland coloured red and the non-Communist island of Taiwan white.

To leave Taiwan white was a major political gaffe, and the stamp designer was accused of being a counter-revolutionary. But a few of his stamps managed to get out to Hongkong, where one was reportedly sold at auction recently for £4,000.

Daily Telegraph, 5/12/81

Does this report suggest that a great change has been taking place in China? Why should an English newspaper give so much space to stamp-collecting in China?

Don't miss it for all the tea in China.

Swan Hellenic art treasures and special interest tours are rather different.

For not only will they lead you through some of the world's most beautiful landscapes. They'll bring you a greater awareness and appreciation of the world's treasures, brought to life by the enthusiasm and in-depth knowledge of our specialist guest lecturers. During a trouble-free journey smoothly arranged by a professional tour manager.

A copy of our tempting brochure can be yours by telephoning us on 01-247 0401, or by sending the coupon.

SWAN HELLENIC
art treasures tours

NAME
ADDRESS

Swan Hellenic Limited, 29-33 Middlesex Street, London E1 7AA.   ATOL 188

Since 1976 China has been visited by many foreign tourists. Are visitors on tours like the one in the advertisement likely to see much of ordinary life in China?

Continuing the story

Where are we now?

During the twentieth century China has always seemed to be changing. The revolution of 1911 ended the rule of the Emperors but it didn't solve China's problems. For the next 40 years different groups — including a foreign power, Japan — fought for control of China.

Since 1949 China has been ruled by new emperors — the leaders of the Chinese Communist Party — but this has meant more changes. Leaders have disagreed about the best policies for China, resulting in upheavals like the Cultural Revolution. China's policies have swung from the left (radical) to the right (moderate) and back again. This kind of change will probably continue.

A rough indication of the swings in the direction of the policies of the Chinese leadership since 1949.

▶ Do you agree with the chart of the pendulum shown below?
▶ Where is the pendulum today – is it moving left or right?
▶ Do these changes affect the lives of ordinary people – are China's basic problems being solved?

Understanding China today

So far this book has told the story of China in the twentieth century. This has been done very quickly, but to understand China today it helps to look back at some events in more detail. Why did things turn out the way they did? How have past events affected China today? The rest of the book investigates important events and questions. Each of them helps to explain why and how China has changed during the twentieth century.

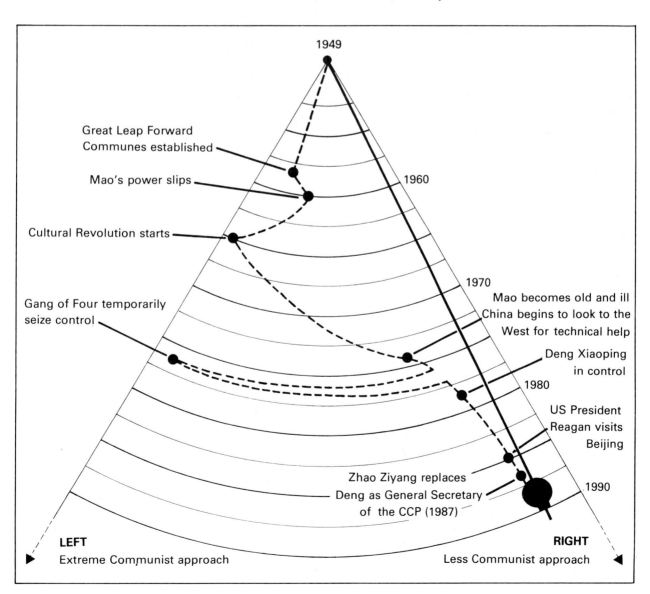

1949

Great Leap Forward
Communes established

Mao's power slips

1960

Cultural Revolution starts

1970

Mao becomes old and ill
China begins to look to the
West for technical help

Gang of Four temporarily
seize control

Deng Xiaoping
in control

1980

US President
Reagan visits
Beijing

Zhao Ziyang replaces
Deng as General Secretary
of the CCP (1987)

1990

LEFT
Extreme Communist approach

RIGHT
Less Communist approach

From Empire to Republic

China was ruled by emperors for four thousand years until 1911. Then there was a revolution. The Manchu emperor was overthrown, and China had to find a new kind of government. This great change in 1911 led to many other changes, so it's important to know why the revolution happened. It will help to explain some of the later developments in China this century.

Why was there a revolution in 1911?

Revolutions don't just happen — they are the result of a variety of causes. Some of these causes had been around in China for a long time, for a hundred years or more. Some causes, however, were fairly new, developing in the late nineteenth century; while some were brand new — they appeared immediately before the revolution.

The cartoon shows how these causes came to work together. On the left are people with very old reasons for wanting revolution. In the middle are people whose reasons developed in the late nineteenth century. On the right, just arriving, are people with new causes. When all these causes came together, the attack on the Manchu dynasty of emperors was successful.

▶ Why did so many people in China want a new government? There are no clues in the cartoon — there's no writing on the rebels' placards! In this section the sources will help to explain why the revolution happened in 1911.

▶ As you look at the sources, work out (1) what the causes were and (2) which causes were:

- long term causes which had been around for over 100 years
- medium-term causes which had developed in the late nineteenth century
- short-term causes which began immediately before the revolution.

Cause 1

SOURCE 1

PARENTS SELLING THEIR CHILDREN   STARVING PEOPLE COMMITTING SUICIDE   "CANNIBALISM"

About 90% of the Chinese people lived in the countryside. During the nineteenth century their conditions worsened — the population grew rapidly, and so many more people went without work and faced starvation. This was made worse when China was hit by natural disasters. Famine and floods probably happened somewhere in China every year until very recently. Food has always been an urgent problem to the Chinese. In fact, the Chinese equivalent to the greeting 'How do you do?' is 'Have you eaten?' Between 1877 and 1879 about 15 million people died because of drought; in 1887–8 another 1 million perished.

Pictures drawn at the end of the nineteenth century showing how desperate some peasants became.

SOURCE 2 — Some taxes paid by the peasants of Gansu Province

Land tax, kettle tax, stocking tax, bedding tax, water-mill tax, copper tax, extraordinary tax, hog tax, penalty tax, door and window tax, army mule tax, skin overcoat tax, temporary expenses tax . . .

When famine hit China in 1907, some foreign governments sent money to help the starving people. This cartoon shows a local governor receiving — and keeping — the money. Would such a cartoon encourage or discourage foreign governments from sending more money to famine victims?

SOURCE 3 — Famine in China, 1876

As the winter drew near, the distress became more acute. Reports came in from villages which previously had forty inhabitants but now had only ten survivors. The price of grain rose rapidly to three and four times its usual rate.

Those who could not afford to leave were forced to pull down their houses and sell every inch of woodwork — doors, windows, frames or rafters — as firewood, and so get money to buy grain to try and keep body and soul together.

To keep warm the poor wretches dug deep pits underground, where twenty, thirty, and even fifty persons would live together. Here the atmosphere, as well as the lack of food, caused a large number of deaths. At first the survivors made two large holes, one for men, the other for women, into which the dead were thrown. Afterwards the dead were left where they fell — there they were devoured by wild dogs, wolves, and vultures . . . I saw men grinding soft stones into powder which was to be mixed with grain, or grass seed or roots, and made into cakes. I tried some of these cakes, and they tasted like what most of them were — clay. Many died of constipation.

For many miles the trees were all white, stripped clean for ten or twenty feet high of their bark, which was used for food.

(adapted from 'Forty-five years in China: Reminiscences', by T. Richard, 1916)

Cause 2

SOURCE 1 — The emperor goes for a walk

Whenever I think of my childhood my head fills with yellow mist. The glazed tiles were yellow; my sedan chair was yellow; my chair cushions were yellow; the linings of my hat and clothes were yellow; the dishes and bowls from which I ate and drank, the material in which my books were wrapped, the window curtains, the bridle of my horse . . . everything was yellow. This colour, the so-called 'brilliant' yellow, was used only by the imperial household and made me feel from my earliest years that I was unique and had a heavenly nature different from that of everybody else.

Whenever I went for a stroll in the garden a procession had to be organised. In front went a eunuch whose function was roughly that of a motor horn; he walked twenty or thirty yards ahead of the rest of the party as a warning to anyone who might be in the area to go away at once. Next came two chief eunuchs walking crabwise on either side of the path; ten paces behind them came the centre of the procession — the Empress Dowager or myself. If I was being carried in a chair there would be two junior eunuchs walking beside me to attend to my wants at any moment. Next came a eunuch with a large silk canopy followed by a large group of eunuchs holding all sorts of things; a seat in case I wanted to rest, changes of clothing, umbrellas and parasols . . . they were followed by eunuchs of the imperial dispensary bearing cases of medicine and first-aid equipment suspended from carrying poles. . . . At the end of the procession came the eunuchs who carried commodes and chamber pots. This procession of several dozen people would proceed in perfect silence and order.

(extract from the autobiography of Aisin Giorro Pu Yi, 'From Emperor to Citizen', 1968)

SOURCE 2

The Empress Ci Xi, who was the real ruler of China for over 40 years. Look at her fingernails, especially on her left hand. Why did she grow them so long that it was difficult to use her fingers?

Ci Xi would not change to fit new ideas. She was given a motor car but it was never used. Why? An Empress could not sit behind a servant and no one had invented a car where the driver was in the back seat!

SOURCE 3

A lingering death for a criminal. The man is imprisoned in this wooden cage with his neck through some planks. He stands on six flat stones. Each day one stone is removed until he strangles.

The Manchu emperors had ruled China since 1644. Even after many small rebellions the emperors failed to make reforms.

▶ *How do the sources that follow help to explain the emperors' refusal to change conditions in China?*

Cause 3

A New Emperor — aged three

For many years the Empress Ci Xi was the real ruler of China, because she dominated her nephew, the Emperor. He had wanted to make reforms in the 1890s, but Ci Xi stopped his plans and put him under house arrest. By the time Ci Xi herself made reforms in the early 1900s they were too little and too late. People now wanted a complete change of government, but Ci Xi remained very powerful. On 14 November 1908 her nephew, the Emperor, died. Next day Ci Xi herself died. The new emperor was a three-year-old boy, Pu Yi. His reign lasted only three years.

The Emperor Pu Yi — ruler of China?

Cause 4

SOURCE 1

Western ideas made the Chinese army think about new weapons and tactics. Many officers were sent abroad for training, often to Japan. This 1911 picture shows the old and the new armies. Would the officers trained abroad want to keep things as they were?

In the nineteenth century more and more Westerners visited China. Most Chinese still thought these visitors were barbarians, uncivilised people of little importance. But some Chinese became worried. They could see how powerful the Westerners were. This made them think about making changes in China.

SOURCE 2 — We should make plans

Because of their knowledge of machinery and mathematics, the nations of the West thrive beyond the seas, reaching the farthest limits of the earth as easily as they move their own fingers and arms. . . . So that our China can stand up to them, we should make plans for commerce and mining; unless we change, they will be rich and we poor. Skills in crafts and manufacturing should be perfected; unless we change, they will be skilful and we clumsy. Steamships, trains and the telegraph should be promoted; unless we change, they will be swift and we slow. Changes in military systems should be studied; unless we change they will be strong and we frail . . .

The Westerners happen to have been the first to catch the winds of change. But are the Westerners to monopolise these secrets? How do we know that within several decades or a century China will not overtake them?

(from 'On Manufacturing Western machines', Feng Gui-fen c. 1860)

▶ *Why did some Chinese want changes?*

Cause 5

SOURCE 1 — Foreign powers 'carve up' China

EN CHINE
Le gâteau des Rois et... des Empereurs

▶ *Try and identify which country each character represents.*

SOURCE 2

By the 1890s many Chinese were resentful of foreign interference in China. This picture shows Chinese attacking pigs, which represent the "foreign devils".

SOURCE 3 — Our race is the greatest, but . . .

We have been invaded by foreign forces, and their control of our economy makes us like prisoners. Now we are unable to fight back. If we want to save China, if we wish to see the Chinese race survive for ever, we must preach nationalism. What is the standing of our race in the world? When we compare all the races in the world, we see that we are the biggest in number, that our race is the greatest and that our history dates back more than 4000 years. But if we do not join together into one strong race, China will be destroyed as a nation and will die!

(adapted from a speech by Sun Yat-sen)

▶ *How did the Chinese react to this foreign control?*
▶ *Whom did they blame?*
▶ *How could they solve the problem?*

Westerners brought many new ideas to China, but they also brought fear. The map shows that large parts of China were controlled by foreign countries.

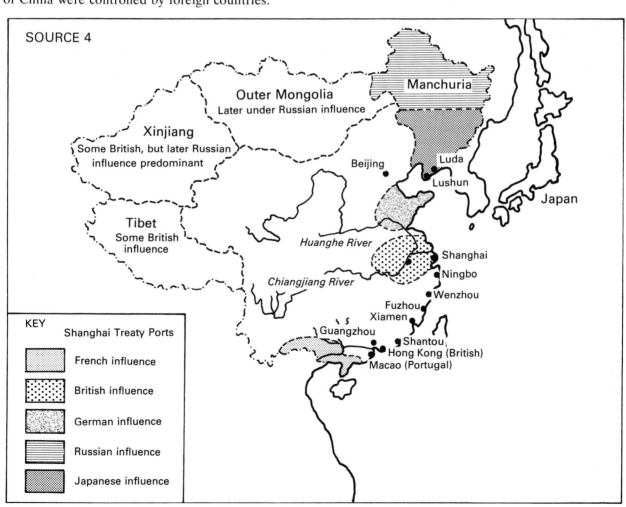

SOURCE 4

Cause 6

The Boxers were members of a secret society who were pledged to 'expel the foreigners' and 'kill all Chinese converts'. At first Ci Xi encouraged this group in their murderous attacks on Westerners in the capital. In 1900 the Boxers attacked the foreign legations in Beijing and a siege began. After two months an international rescue force arrived and the Boxer rebels were rounded up and many thousands were executed. Ci Xi disowned them and agreed to pay the foreign governments 450 million dollars in compensation.

SOURCE

The Boxer Rebellion was cruelly suppressed as Western armies rooted out the leaders. Western countries forced the Chinese government to sign an agreement, giving the Westerners even more power. So, the Boxer Rebellion ended with increased power for the hated "barbarians". However, the rebellion did shock many Chinese scholars in to believing that the Manchu rulers were to blame for the foreign control in China, so they must be overthrown.

Cause 7

SOURCE — An explosion in Hankou

An Australian journalist's report of the events on 9 October 1911.

Still no date had been set for the revolution. Then, on 9 October 1911, just as twilight settled over the sprawling city of Hankou, men gathered in a rain-washed house. It was rebel headquarters. They sat down in the barren room on the top floor to discuss, as they had for nights on end, the business of revolution, the business of despatching the Manchus into a hell of obscurity. In the basement below, men were at work on the technical side of the problem. They were making bombs.

In the conference room, Huang Xing said, 'We should be ready by the end of the month.'

A slight, sharp-eyed youth protested: 'But we lack army and arms. We are only a handful.' He added reverently, 'Our great leader — Dr Sun — What has he to say?'

Huang answered quickly, 'Dr Sun? We don't know where he is. But never fear, we are on the verge of being ready.'

A few minutes later, an ear-splitting explosion shook the house violently and broke windows across the street. One of their bombs had exploded accidentally. Several buildings away, a German butcher was about to close his shop. Frightened, he telephoned the police. Before they arrived, Huang and his men had departed. They knew police would find their bomb factory. It was night now, and they hurried across the river to Wuzhang, leaving behind in their haste the seal of the 'republic' and a list of all the conspirators.

At Wuzhang, the word was whispered that rebellion was inescapable, and in the grey light of morning the rebels took the long dangerous step from which there would be no return. They shot the Manchu garrison sentries and marched into the quarters of the commanding officer, Colonel Li Yuan-hong.

('Donald of China', Earl A. Selle, 1948)

Cause 8

Sun Yat-sen, photographed in 1914.

SOURCE 1 — An Englishman meets Sun Yat-sen

I was shown into a room, and as I entered, a short young man dressed in European clothes stepped forward, from a table around which were seated a number of Chinamen in native costume, with outstretched hand to greet me . . . he was slightly built, with pointed black moustache and bright, dark eyes. His manner was brisk, and the grasp of his hand was firm.

Seldom have I met a more interesting personality. There was that inexplicable something about him that stamped him as a leader of men, a personal magnetism about him that affected one strangely, a singleness of purpose to the end for which he was devoting his life that compelled admiration . . . Sun Yat-sen wishes to change the Imperial rule; and, as he said, the times are ripening for the change, when the foreigners have looted the capital, outraged the gods, and when the Emperor has been shattered and the sacred precincts of the palace itself in the heart of Beijing desecrated by the feet of invaders.

(from 'Two Western Orientals', quoted in Sun Yat-sen, Lyon Sharman, 1934)

SOURCE 2 — Long live the Chinese Republic!

The single goal of revolution is to sweep away thousands of years of slavery and wash away the terrible humiliation of 260 years of Manchu cruelty, so that China will be cleansed. We Chinese were enslaved by the Manchus, the Europeans and the Americans. Two thousand years ago we were all slaves, and now, 2000 years later, we are still all slaves . . . Citizens of China! I wish my fellow people would all unite together with one heart, exert all their energies, urge one another on to end your deep-rooted servility, and move forward to become citizens of China.

Compatriots of the great Han race, men and women of all ages! be revolutionary: each and every one of you, look upon this revolution as your duty, as necessary as daily food and drink! Your land occupies two-thirds of the Asian continent, your compatriots comprise one-fifth of the world's population. Your tea is more than enough to supply beverage for all the millions of the people of the world, and your coal can supply the whole world with fuel for 2000 years. You have government; administer it yourselves. You have laws; keep them yourselves. You have industries; run them yourselves. You have land; protect it yourselves. You have natural resources; you should exploit them yourselves. Attack your hereditary foe, the Manchus. Then wipe out the foreign devils who have infringed upon your sovereignty. . .

> Long live the revolutionary independence of the great Han people!
> Long live the Chinese Republic!
> Long live the freedom of the 400,000,000 compatriots of the Chinese Republic!

(from 'The Revolutionary Army', Zou Rong, 1903)

Why did the revolution begin?

▶ *All the causes you have looked at over the last few pages helped to start the 1911 Revolution. Which of them were the most important — the long-term causes, or immediate events like the explosion at Hankou?*

▶ *Why did the revolution start in 1911, not 1908 or earlier?*

▶ *Once you have decided on a list of causes, devise a flow diagram to show how one cause led on to another until the 1911 Revolution broke out.*

Who is to govern China — the GMD or the CCP?

The revolution of 1911 did not decide who would rule China. For almost 40 years there was uncertainty and confusion until the Chinese Communist Party (CCP) won control. During these years a struggle developed between Guomindang (GMD) and CCP to win the support of the Chinese people. Winning enough support wasn't easy. For example, the CCP's ideas might win the support of one group of people, but the same ideas would put off another group. People might support the GMD at one time, and then switch their support to the CCP.

On the chart are the different kinds of supporters the GMD and CCP wanted.

▶ *Which groups would be more likely to support the GMD? Which groups would be more likely to support the CCP?*
▶ *Would any groups be uncertain whom to support, or likely to change from one group to another?*
▶ *Why do you think they would support these parties?*

Eighty per cent of China's population was made up of poor peasants under the control of landowners.

The Chinese Population in 1911

Class	Percentage of population
The poor peasants did not own their own land, and had to pay heavy rents and taxes to the landlords. Desperately poor and illiterate, they were vulnerable to disease, drought, flood and famine.	80%
The richer peasants by contrast were quite well off, and employed other peasants to work on their farms.	4%
The industrial workers mostly worked long hours for low pay in very bad conditions. There were only a few factories in China, mainly near the coast. The workers lived in very poor and overcrowded conditions, and had barely enough food.	6%
The Chinese merchants were a small group, but very rich and powerful. They realised, however, that trade was in the hands of foreign countries, such as Britain, France, Japan and the USA, and that this was reducing their profits and their power.	2%
The landowners were another small but very rich and powerful group. They lived in luxury in the countryside, collecting taxes from the peasants. They sometimes held official posts in their area.	2%
Army officers had considerable power and responsibility, but were not regularly paid. Their supplies were not well organised either, and they were often left to find their own billets and food.	2%
Intellectuals and scholars were very few in number, but had great influence. Most wanted China to be united, and to have a strong government to build up her power in the world.	2%

In addition to the Chinese people, there were the representatives of foreign governments. They wanted peace and stability in China without delay, so that their firms could trade with the Chinese without hindrance.

The Guomindang

Chiang Kai-shek

Born in 1887, in a village 160 km (100 ml) south of Shanghai.

Background: Chiang came from a prosperous merchant and landowning family.

Education: Chiang was taught by a private tutor, and then went to the Military Academy in Tokyo.

Early career:

1917	military adviser to Sun Yat-sen in Guangzhou
1918-21	stockbroker in Shanghai, where he made several friends among rich businessmen
1923	visited Moscow to study at Russia's military training school for the GMD
1925	became leader of the GMD on the death of Sun Yat-sen

National Reconstruction

The GMD wanted the revolution to lead the 'National Reconstruction' of China's economic and military power. What this means is explained by Sun Yat-sen, the founder and leader of the GMD, in a speech to the party's First National Congress in 1924.

SOURCE 1 — The Three People's Principles of Sun Yat-sen

The National Government shall reconstruct the Republic of China on the basis of the revolutionary Three People's Principles.

The first task of reconstruction is the people's livelihood. The government should, in cooperation with the people, strive together to provide the four great necessities of the people — food, clothing, shelter and means of travel.

Second is the people's sovereignty. The government should train and direct the people in political knowledge and to enable them to exercise the powers of election . . .

Third comes nationalism. The government should help and guide the small racial groups in China towards self-government. It should offer resistance to foreign aggression and revise foreign treaties to give us equality with other trading nations.

(from a speech given by Sun Yat-sen in 1924, quoted in 'The China Handbook', 1937–43)

This statement originally formed the basis of GMD policy, but when Chiang became leader the emphasis began to change. More stress was put on building a strong, unified, prosperous China with no foreign interference. Improving the ordinary people's lives was now less important.

Chiang Kai-shek.

SOURCE 2 — The importance of unity

In order to make China powerful, China must be unified. In order to unify China, the warlords must be eliminated. In order to eliminate the warlords, the armed forces must be organised. In order to organise the armed forces a military academy must be established.

(from a report by Chiang Kai-shek quoted in 'A Brief History of the Chinese National Revolutionary Forces', Hu Pu-yu, 1972)

SOURCE 3 — Land policy

We propose that the government shall buy back the land from the landowners, if necessary, according to the price of the land and the amount of land tax. . . As a result, neither the government nor the landowner will lose.

(from a speech given by Sun Yat-sen in 1924, quoted in 'The China Handbook 1937–43')

SOURCE 4 — Views on liberty

If we speak of liberty to the average man he surely will not understand us. The reason why the Chinese really have attached no importance to liberty is because the idea is a new one in China.

We have no cohesion; we are 'loose sand'. Because we have been 'loose sand' we have been invaded by foreign powers. If we want to throw off foreign aggression we shall have to add cement to the 'loose sand' so as to make solid stone.

The liberty of the individual must not be too great, but that of the nation must be unlimited.

(from a speech of Sun Yat-sen, quoted in 'The Rise of Communist China', J. Kennett, 1970)

The Chinese Communist Party

Mao Zedong

Mao Zedong

Born in 1893, in Hunan Province
Background: Mao's parents were well-off farmers
Education: Mao went to the village school, and then attended a teacher-training school in Zhangsha
Early career:

1918   Assistant librarian at a university, where he began reading the works of Marx and learning about the 1917 Russian Revolution
1921   became Communist Party organiser in factories and mines
1926   became head of the Peasant Department of the CCP, investigating the problems of the peasants
1927   organised uprisings among the peasants
1935   elected leader of the Chinese Communist Party

SOURCE 1 — Mao's attitude to revolutionary violence

A revolution is not a dinner party, or writing an essay, or painting a picture, or doing embroidery; it cannot be so leisurely and gentle. A revolution is an act of violence by which one class overthrows another. A rural revolution is a revolution by which the peasants overthrow the power of the feudal landlord class; without using the greatest force, the peasants cannot possibly overthrow the deep-rooted authority of the landlords, which has lasted for thousands of years!

(Mao Zedong 'Selected Works', 1927)

SOURCE 2 — The importance of the mass movement of peasants

The present upsurge of the peasant movement is a colossal event. In a very short time several hundred million peasants will rise like a mighty storm, like a hurricane, a force so swift and violent that no power, however great, will be able to hold it back. They will sweep all the imperialists, warlords, corrupt officials, local tyrants and evil landlords into their graves.

Every revolutionary comrade will be put to the test. There are three alternatives: to march at their head and lead them. To trail behind them, waving your arms and criticising. Or to stand in their way and oppose them. Events will force you to make your choice quickly.

(extracts from 'The Thoughts of Mao Zedong', 1927)

SOURCE 3 — The CCP attitude to land ownership

Redistribution of land was one of the main principles of communist policy. It provided for the confiscation of all landlords' land and the confiscation of all land of rich peasants that was not cultivated by the owners themselves. The poorest farmers and farm labourers were all then to be provided with land enough for a livelihood.

('Red Star over China', E. Snow, 1957)

SOURCE 4 — Mao's attitude to the army

Mao believed that the CCP needed their own army — The Red Army. To start with it was composed of landless peasants, deserters and bandits. It was based in the remote areas of the countryside, and they used guerrilla tactics. He summed up these tactics in this way.

When the enemy advances, we retreat.
When the enemy camps, we harass.
When the enemy tires, we attack.
When the enemy retreats, we pursue.

SOURCE 5 — Liu Shao-ji on Communism

Is a communist world good or not? We all know that it is very good. In such a world there will be no exploiters, oppressors, landlords, capitalists, imperialists or fascists. There will be no oppressed and exploited people, no darkness, ignorance, backwardness. . . . Can communist society be brought about? Our answer is 'yes'. The ultimate result of the class struggle of mankind is that such a society will inevitably be brought about.

(from 'How to be a good Communist', Liu Shao-ji, 1939)

Fighting between the CCP and the GMD

SOURCE 1

Communists executed by the GMD in Guangzhou.

SOURCE 2 — Violence in Guanzhou in 1927

The Communist plan was for a rebellion in Guangzhou, with a general peasant uprising. Confusion had seized the city, rebel squads and aimless crowds surged in the streets. The killing was brutal and indiscriminate, but anti-communist forces were soon to achieve 'an eye for and eye and a tooth for a tooth' revenge.

For identification the communists wore a red sash and red ties; the weather was warm, and as the wearers perspired the dye discoloured their necks.

Communist forces held Guangzhou for two days. Then Zhang Fak-wei's 'Ironsides' opened the attack. When the communists saw that they were losing the fight, they began discarding sashes and ties, but the tell-tale dye-stains would not wipe off.

'Execution squads patrolled the streets', reported an American diplomat, 'I saw a rickshaw stopped, the man grabbed by the police, his shirt jerked from his neck disclosing the red stain. He was pushed to the side of the road, forced to kneel down, and shot while the crowd of people in the street applauded!'

According to another American embassy official 'Two lots of 500 and 1000 men were each taken out and machine gunned. Realising this was a waste of ammunition, the soldiers took the victims down river in boats and pushed them overboard in lots of ten or twelve men tied together. The slaughter continued for four or five days during which some 6000 people, allegedly Communists, lost their lives in the city of Guangzhou.'

(adapted from 'Chinese Communism', R. C. North, 1969)

▶ The passers by in the street seem unconcerned at the presence of these bodies. Why might this be so? Suggest all the reasons you can.
▶ Can you be sure this caption is accurate and describes the photograph? How would you begin to check that this photograph shows what the caption says it does?

During the years of the GMD (Nationalist) government little was done to lighten the burden of the peasants. They continued to pay 65% of their income in various forms of tax. When famine struck between 1929 and 1932, millions died.

SOURCE 3 — The plight of the peasants

Here for the first time in my life I came upon men who were dying because they had nothing to eat. Children are even more pitiable, with their little skeletons bent over and misshapen, their crooked bones, their little arms like twigs, and their bellies, filled with bark and sawdust, protruding like tumours. I don't mean to dramatise horror. These are things I saw myself and I shall never forget.

The most shocking thing was that in many of those towns there were still rich men, rice hoarders, moneylenders and landlords, with armed guards to defend them, while they profiteered enormously. The shocking thing was that in the cities — where officials danced or played with singsong girls — there was grain and food, and had been for months.

(from 'Red Star over China', Edgar Snow, 1937)

▶ If you were a GMD official how might you defend the GMD record? List the reasons why you were unable to do more to improve the lives of ordinary people.

49

The Long March

Why did the CCP undertake the Long March?

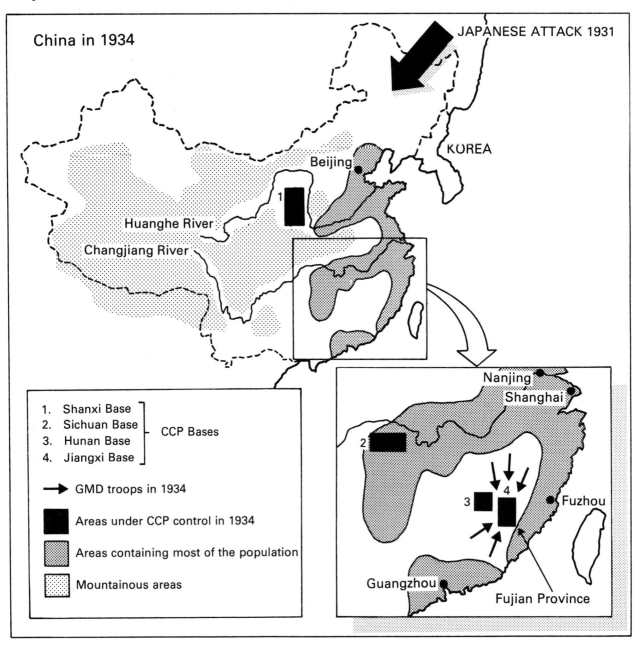

China in 1934

JAPANESE ATTACK 1931

KOREA

Beijing

Huanghe River

Changjiang River

1. Shanxi Base
2. Sichuan Base   CCP Bases
3. Hunan Base
4. Jiangxi Base

→ GMD troops in 1934

■ Areas under CCP control in 1934

▨ Areas containing most of the population

░ Mountainous areas

Nanjing
Shanghai

Fuzhou

Guangzhou

Fujian Province

The situation in 1934

In 1934 most of China was under the control of the
GMD with their capital at Nanjing. The CCP
controlled only four small bases, mainly in remote
rural areas of China. The CCP had tried to keep
control of several towns, but the GMD had ruthlessly
driven them out. Jiangxi base in the south was by far
the strongest and best organised CCP base. It was in
Jiangxi that Mao Zedong was one of the leaders.
However, Mao was not in total control and there were
many who disagreed with him. One CCP leader from
Shanghai, called Li Li-san, escaped to the Jiangxi
base, but he always hoped to return to the coastal
towns to start a revolution.

Chiang was determined to destroy the Jiangxi base.
He had previously launched four 'extermination
campaigns' but, despite bitter fighting and heavy
losses on both sides, he had failed to dislodge the CCP
from their mountain retreat.

In October 1933 Chiang began a blockade of Jiangxi.
Forts and blockhouses were built along the roads into
the base to stop the movement of essential supplies.
With an army of 700,000 men Chiang encircled the
CCP and waited for them to surrender.

What were the CCP to do?

There was much discussion in the CCP about the best course of action. Should they abandon their foothold in the more important south of the country? Should they move away and try to rebuild somewhere else?

▶ *What would you have done?*

Here are the options. Consider each carefully:

A Stand and fight.
B Surrender to the GMD.
C Break out of Jiangxi and head for the towns.
D Break out of Jiangxi and head for the countryside.
E Arrange a truce with the GMD (perhaps in order to jointly fight the invading Japanese).
F Unite with the neighbouring province of Fujian, which was rebelling.
G Try to break the blockade in some other way, such as by sending messages for help to other CCP bases.

▶ *Put yourself in the position of a leading member of the CCP in Jiangxi in 1934. In view of the situation, which would be the best option for the CCP?*

Before making your decision, consider the following points:

1 The CCP base in Jiangxi had been in existence for seven years. It covered a large area in mountainous country, and was fairly easy to defend. The base contained over 1 million people, including a Red Army of nearly 300,000 men. It was well organised, with cooperative farms and education for the peasants. Committees had been set up to take decisions in the interests of the community.

2 The Japanese were beginning to take advantage of the confusion and the fighting in China. In 1931 Japan had begun to advance into China's provinces in the far north. In February 1932 the Jiangxi base declared war on Japan as if it were a separate country.

3 The GMD government had done little for the people in the west of China. The peasants were still mostly ruled by cruel landlords. They were downtrodden and in a rebellious mood.

4 In the neighbouring province of Fujian the 19th Route Army was in revolt against Chiang's leadership. Together with a group of politicians, it had set up a rebel provincial government. Fujian province had access to the sea.

5 From their action against the CCP in the towns, the GMD seemed determined to destroy the CCP totally and so remove any threat to their authority in China. (See Source 2 — Violence In Guangzhou, p 49)

A recent painting, showing Mao in 1934 in Jiangxi. How reliable do you think this picture is as evidence?

The events of the Long March

Break out from Jiangxi

By October 1934, the GMD forces were closing in on Ruijing, the Jiangxi base capital. Desertion from the Red Army increased, and it is said some even committed suicide for fear of what the GMD might do to them. The Jiangxi base had to be surrendered, and as many as possible would have to fight their way out. Twenty thousand wounded would have to be left behind with the local peasants. The children of the soldiers who went were also left. Mao Zedong left his own two children behind, and they were never heard of again.

The factories and military arsenals were stripped — much equipment was buried, the rest was put on the backs of mules and donkeys. They carried everything, including sewing machines, printing presses, heavy weapons, tons of documents and bags of silver Mexican dollars. The Red Army was young and well disciplined, but its task was formidable. In the end, about 100,000 men broke out of Jiangxi base through the GMD lines of forts and blockhouses. The slaughter was terrible — nearly half the men were killed.

▶ *The GMD troops thought they had won an important battle, but later the communists hailed this as the start of the heroic Long March. Was it a heroic start?*

SOURCE 1 — A Veteran of the Long March remembers

Well, we ourselves at the beginning did not know that we were actually on the Long March, and that it was going to be such a big thing. All we knew was that we were getting out of the bases; we were surrounded and being choked; a million men against us, tanks, aeroplanes . . . defeat after defeat. We broke through one ring of fortification, then a second, then a third, and we marched through the late autumn and early winter, westward, always westward, with the rain soaking us to the skin and the wind in our faces. . .

We were about a hundred thousand in number, and very visible, a long, slow caravan. Every day we were attacked, front and back and both sides, by GMD armies and local warlords' armies; and we fought them and defeated them, and went on, but every time many of us died; and then we got to Zunyi in January of 1935. There we held a big conference, to study our further moves, to assess our losses.

(from an interview with Han Suyin, 'The Crippled Tree', 1965)

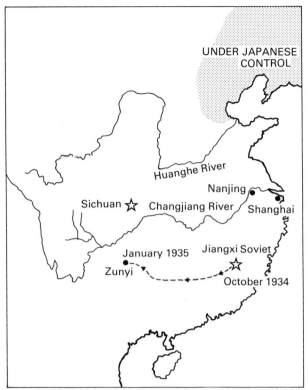

The first stage of the Long March, October 1934 - January 1935.

Zunyi Conference

The Zunyi Conference became a turning point in the Long March. Now that the Red Army was deep in the Chinese countryside it was decided that they would be better off with a man of the people, a genuine peasant leader, and Mao Zedong was elected. His full title was 'Chairman of the Military Committee of the CCP'. Mao criticised the short-sighted leadership of those who had concentrated resources in the Jiangxi base. He encouraged the main Red Army to link up with another section of the Red Army (the Fourth Front Army) in their Sichuan base. He spurred them to march on, with the patriotic slogan 'Let's go north and fight the Japanese'.

The building at Zunyi where the Communists met.

Crossing the Changjiang River

Chiang Kai-shek's forces blocked the way north to the Sichuan base so Mao led the Red Army in a wide westward sweep, hoping somehow to cross the wide Changjiang and then link up with the Fourth Front Army. It was not certain that they could achieve this, let alone survive in these wild remote areas in the foothills of Tibet.

The GMD leaders knew that the river would have to be crossed by the Red Army — but they did not know where. They ordered all ferry boats to be kept moored on the north bank and sent out a detachment of GMD troops to attack the Red Army from the rear. The Reds managed to keep their enemy guessing. The main force stopped on the south bank and began to construct a bridge as though preparing for a crossing. A small group was sent on a forced march for 135 km (85 ml) to capture ferry boats from a crossing place on the Jinsha River. They completed the march in 36 hours. Some dressed in GMD uniforms and shouted to the GMD guards on the north bank to send over a boat. They then crossed the river, attacked the guards and captured another five boats. In the next nine days and nights the entire Red Army was ferried across in small groups in these few boats. They then burned the boats. It was another two days before the main GMD army arrived on the scene.

The GMD leaders were not dismayed by this success. In fact it appeared that the CCP were caught in a more dangerous trap. One GMD general said: 'Behind them is the Jinsha River. Ahead of them is the Dadu River. They are caught like fish in a bottle. Now is the time to annihilate the Red Bandits.'

Furthermore, the Red Army were now in an area where a wild and unfriendly tribe — the Lolos — lived. The Lolos people did not welcome the Red Army, and it was only after they had been bribed with money and weapons that the army columns were allowed through. It is also said that one Red Army commander drank the blood of a chicken to become a blood brother of the tribe.

This picture is copied from a book printed by the Chinese authorities in Beijing titled "Recalling the Long March". It is an account of the March by a Red Army soldier who took part. It is written as an heroic adventure story, and is illustrated with pictures showing the Red Army's famous triumph. In this picture, entitled "Capturing Ferry Boats on Jinsha River". How are the GMD soldiers portrayed? Does the picture indicate the Red Army had any difficulty in capturing the ferries? Are there any other aspects of the incident shown here which you could question?

A Lolos tribesman.

Crossing the Dadu River

Another great obstacle now faced the Red Army —
the Dadu River had to be crossed. The river was
swollen with the water from the spring thaw, and
GMD troops controlled all crossing points. At first
they seized ferry boats, but they came under fierce
attack from the GMD air force. A new crossing point
had to be captured. A daring plan was hatched to send
a Red Army regiment on a forced march of 160 km
(100 ml) along steep mountain paths to capture the
Luding suspension bridge over the river. They
completed the march in just two days, arriving at the
southern end of the bridge in the early morning of the
third day. The bridge was made of thirteen iron chains
slung out across the gorge. Wooden planks formed a
walkway across, and there were chains on either side
as hand rails. When the Red Army soldiers arrived
they found to their dismay that the bridge was heavily
guarded on the far bank and the wooden planks had
been ripped up from the first half of the bridge. It is
said that there was no shortage of volunteers for the
first assault, and from among them twenty-two were
selected.

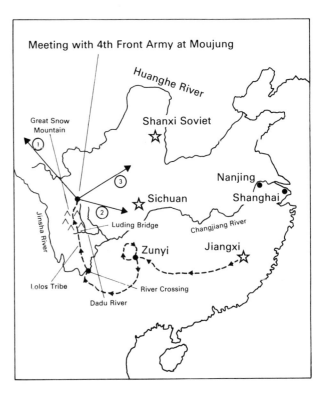

The progress of the Red Army, from Zunyi to the meeting with
the Fourth Front Army.

SOURCE 2 — Taking the Luding bridge

Platoon Commander Ma Dajin stepped out, grasped
one of the chains, and began swinging hand-over-
hand towards the north bank. The platoon political
director followed, and after him the men. As they
swung along, Red Army machine guns laid down a
protecting screen of fire, and the Engineering Corps
began bringing up tree trunks and laying the bridge
flooring. The army watched breathlessly as the men
swung along the bridge chains. Ma Dajin was the
first to be shot into the wild torrent below. Then
another man and another. The others pushed along,
but just before they reached the flooring at the north
bridgehead they saw enemy soldiers dumping cans
of kerosene on the planks and setting them on fire.
Watching the sheet of flame spread, some men
hesitated, but the platoon political leader at last
sprang down on the flooring calling to the others to
follow they came and crouched on the planks,
releasing their hand grenades and unbuckling their
swords.

They ran through the flames and threw their hand
grenades into the midst of the enemy. More and
more men followed, the flames lapping at their
clothing. Behind them sounded the roar of their
comrades, and beneath the roar they heavy THUD,
THUD, THUD, of the last tree trunks falling into place.
The bridge became a mass of running men with rifles
ready, tramping out the flames as they ran.

(from an interview with Agnes Smedley, an American
reporter)

The Luding Suspension Bridge.

Fewer than fifty men were lost in the attack, although
many were burned or wounded, and in two hours the
GMD troops defending the bridge were beaten. The
Red Army could continue its march north.

The Great Snow Mountain

The aim was to link up with the Fourth Front Army from the Sichuan base. High mountain ranges had to be crossed. The first was the Great Snow Mountain (4800m high) — even in June many of the poorly dressed southerners died of exposure.

SOURCE 3 — The Great Snow Mountain

The Great Snow Mountain is blanketed in eternal snow. There are great glaciers and everything is white and silent. . . Heavy fogs swirled about us, there was a high wind, and half-way up it began to rain. As we climbed higher and higher we were caught in a terrible hailstorm, and the air became so thin we could hardly breathe. Speech was completely impossible, and the cold so dreadful that our breath froze and our hands and lips turned blue. Men and animals staggered and fell into chasms, and disappeared for ever. Those who sat down to rest or to relieve themselves froze to death on the spot. It rained, then snowed, and the fierce wind whipped our bodies and more men died. Hundreds of men died there. . . All along the route, we kept reaching down to pull men to their feet, only to find that they were already dead.

(from an interview with Agnes Smedley)

Snow in June, a painting of the Red Army on the Great Snow Mountain. In what ways does this tell a different story from Source 3? Why is it different?

The meeting with the Fourth Front Army

The main body of the Red Army led by Mao met up with the Fourth Front Army, which had moved out of the Sichuan base, at the village of Moujung. Zhang Guo-dao led the Fourth Front Army, and a disagreement flared up about which direction the combined armies should now take. There were three options:

1 **Zhang Guo-dao's First Plan:** They should head for the remote province of Xinjiang in the West, crossing over desert and mountains. This was a very safe area, and close to Soviet Russia from which they could obtain supplies.

2 **Zhang Guo-dao's Second Plan:** They should return to Sichuan province, his home area, and drive out the GMD there. They were likely to get much local support, and Sichuan was closer to the centre of the action.

3 **Mao Zedong's Plan:** They should head for Shaanxi province, where a weak CCP base was already established. To get there they would have to cross wild country and treacherous grassland swamp. Shaanxi was remote, and close to areas recently invaded by the Japanese.

▶ *Which option would you favour? Why?*

The Qinghai Grasslands

The rest of the Red Army leaders accepted Mao's plan. Mao had said that to go back to Sichuan would risk being caught 'like a turtle in a jar', and Xinjiang was too remote. But by heading north the army had to cross the Qinghai Grasslands — a mixture of marsh and quicksand where it rains for eight or nine months a year.

SOURCE 4 — Crossing the grasslands

Huge clumps of grass grew on dead clumps beneath them. . . No tree or shrub grew here, no bird ventured near, no insect sounded. There was not even a stone. There was nothing, nothing but endless stretches of grass. . .

The water underfoot looked like horses' urine and gave off a smell which made people vomit. Mosquitoes bit until our faces went as black as a negro's and our bodies became weaker and weaker.

Between the clumps the soil was very soft and loose, and if you took a step you would sink down at least 18 inches (45cm). Sometimes there were bottomless pools of mud. If you weren't careful, and took a false step, a man and his horse would sink down; the more they struggled, the deeper they would go; and if no one pulled them out that was the end of them. Men had to sleep standing up in pairs or groups of four, back to back — or else drown in the swamp.   (from an interview with Agnes Smedley)

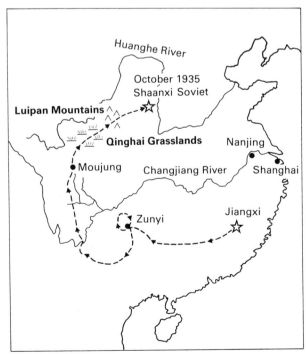

The final stretch of the Long March. The Red Army reaches Shaanxi.

The end of the Long March

More battles were fought, and the Liupan Mountains crossed, before the remnants of the Red Army reached the Shaanxi CCP base in October 1935. The estimates of the number of soldiers that survived varies. Some say 30,000 out of the original 100,000 finished the march. Others say as few as 5000 completed it. Mao Zedong's orderly recounted the welcome the Red Army received like this:

SOURCE 5 — Entering Shaanxi

We heard the beatings of gongs and drums, and the noise of a crowd of people. From a distance we could see a large gathering . . . at the entrance to the village. The people were waiting to welcome the Chairman. As soon as they caught sight of him, they cheered madly. Amidst a tremendous din of gongs and drums, the crowd rushed up, waving small red and green banners bearing the words 'Welcome Chairman Mao — Welcome the Red Army — Expand the Shaanxi Soviet Area — Smash the Enemy's Encirclement Campaign — Long Live the Chinese Communist Party'.

SOURCE 6

Drawings of relics from the Long March which have been preserved. Why do you think they have been preserved?

Assessing the Long March

The GMD view

Histories of China written from the GMD point of view don't call this event the Long March. It is not often mentioned but when it is it is referred to as the Great Retreat or the 25,000 Li Pursuit.

▶ *Are either of these names justified?*
▶ *How could this event be seen as a GMD victory?*

SOURCE 1 — The Great Retreat

In the autumn of 1934, after the fifth siege laid by the Chinese Government forces, the communists broke the siege and fled to the west. With some 100,000 people under their control, the communist remnants began the long westward trek on 16 October. . .

The enemy was routed and fled to northern Shaanxi. By this time their exhausted force of 2000 to 3000 men was completely helpless. The government forces completed the long-distance campaign to press and annihilate the enemy. At last, the provinces of the south-west were unified under government control.

('Brief History of Chinese National Revolutionary Forces', Bu-you Zhong Wu Publishing Co., Taiwan, 1971)

Mao's verdict on the Long March. Do you think this was how other people saw the Long March?

The CCP view

The CCP viewed the march completely differently. This is a typical assessment from one of the many communist books written about it.

SOURCE 2

The courage and endurance shown by the Red Army men fully demonstrates the unstoppable vitality of the communist movement and the all-conquering fighting strength of the army led by the Communist Party.

('Recalling the Long March', Liu Po-cheng)

Mao's verdict

In December 1935 Mao made a speech in which he gave his view of the Long March, and its importance in the history of the Communist revolution in China.

▶ *Do you think his description of the Long March (Source 3) is accurate?*

SOURCE 3 — Mao's account of the Long March

The Long March is the first of its kind in history. Has history ever witnessed a long march such as ours? For twelve months we were under daily reconnaissance and bombing from the skies by scores of planes, while on land we were encircled and pursued, obstructed and intercepted by a huge force of several hundred thousand men. We encountered untold difficulties and dangers on the way, yet by using our two legs we swept across a distance of more than twenty thousand li (10,500 km; 6500 ml) through the length and breadth of eleven provinces. Let us ask, has history ever known a long march to equal ours?

No, never. The Long March is a message. It has shown the world that the Red Army is an army of heroes, while Chiang Kai-shek and his like are powerless. It has proclaimed their utter failure to encircle, pursue, obstruct and intercept us. The Long March is also propaganda. It has announced to 200 million people in eleven provinces that the road of the Red Army is their only road to liberation. Without the Long March, how could the broad masses have learned so quickly about the existence of the great truth which the Red Army embodies? The Long March is also a seeding-machine. In the eleven provinces it has sown many seeds which will sprout, leaf, blossom and bear fruit, and will yield a harvest in the future. In a word, the Long March has ended with victory for us and defeat for the enemy.

Why did the Communists defeat the GMD?

SOURCE 1

Chiang Kai-shek with President Roosevelt and Churchhill at the wartime Cairo conference held in 1943. Does this suggest that the GMD was likely to be defeated by the CCP?

SOURCE 2

Looking back, it seems that as early as 1946 the defeat of the GMD was inevitable. Yet, right up to the end of 1948, the best informed and most impartial observers hesitated to predict the complete victory of Mao Zedong. Many still hoped for a partition of China, as had once occurred centuries before.

But at the outset Mao's chances of success were very slim. Clearly outclassed in numbers and supplies, he dominated only a small territory; he had no money, no resources, no allies. Opposing Mao was a man to whom propaganda had given the stature of a giant, a prospective member of President Roosevelt's world-governing Big Four, the master of more than three hundred and fifty million people, of war-hardened armies, of enormous stocks of modern military supplies. Between these two champions, who could have hesitated in choosing the eventual victor?

(adapted from 'Republican China', Ed. by F. Schunnan and O. Schnell, 1967)

The conflict between the Red Army and the GMD went through many phases between 1925 and 1949. There were times of full-scale civil war, times when the Red Army and the GMD fought together against foreign enemies, times when the Red Army was forced to retreat and seemed beaten. Yet in 1949 the communist Red Army was victorious and the GMD led by Chiang Kai-shek fled to the offshore island of Taiwan.

▶ *Was a victory for the Red Army expected?*

▶ *Why then, if the GMD seemed to be in such a superior position, did they lose in 1949? You may already have some ideas; the following pages provide more evidence about the two sides' armies, their attitude to the peasants and the Japanese occupation and the two sides' leaders.*

▶ *After studying and discussing the evidence, draw up a list of reasons for the CCP victory.*

Comparing the CCP and GMD
1 — The army

SOURCE 1 — Relative Strength of Red Army and GMD Forces 1945–1949

American Estimates	Red Army (1000's)	GMD (1000's)	Ratio
July 1946	1000	3000	1:3
June 1947	1150	2700	1:2.35
Beginning 1948	1150	2723	1:2.37
February 1949	1622	1500	1:0.92
CCP Estimates	Red Army (1000's)	GMD (1000's)	Ratio
July 1946	1278	4300	1:3.36
June 1947	1950	3730	1:1.9
June 1948	2800	3650	1:1.3
June 1949	4000	1500	1:0.37

Two views of the strength of the two armies. Why were the estimates sometimes different and sometimes the same? How do these estimates explain America's belief that the GMD would win?

SOURCE 2 — The Red Army

From the highest commander down to the rank and file these men ate and dressed alike. There was very little difference in living quarters of commanders and men, and they passed freely back and forth without any formality. The Red Army was so often the only side in a battle that believed it was fighting for something. When not in the trenches or on outpost duty, the Red soldiers observed a six-day week. The schedule of the day included: an hour's exercise immediately after rising; breakfast; two hours of military drill; two hours of political lectures and discussion; lunch; an hour of rest; two hours of character study; two hours of games and sports; dinner; songs and group meetings.

There was a wall newspaper in every club, and a committee of soldiers was responsible for keeping it up to date. A typical one included daily and weekly notices of the Communist Party, radio bulletins of Red Army victories, new songs to be learned and, perhaps most interestingly, two sections called red and white columns, devoted respectively to praise and criticism. 'Praise' consisted of tributes to the courage, bravery and unselfishness of individuals or groups. In the other column, comrades lashed into each other and their officers (by name) for such things as failure to keep a rifle clean, slackness in study, losing a hand grenade or bayonet, or smoking on duty.

(Edgar Snow, 1936)

SOURCE 3 — The GMD

The basis of all conscription was bribery and influence. Some of the rich never entered the army; some of the poor could never escape. Officers considered it their privilege and right to beat soldiers. During both the Japanese and the civil war, I saw soldiers beaten on station platforms with bamboo rods, on highways with automobile crank handles, in rooms with iron bars. There were some kindly officers who called their troops 'their younger brothers'. But, on the whole, the life of the ordinary soldier was just above a pig and just below a mule.

Soldiers, if wounded, had small chance of living. Time and again I have seen wounded soldiers thrown off trains because they did not have the price of a ticket; wounded men thrown off half-empty trucks because an officer and brutal sergeant wanted to transport opium — thrown off, mind you, not into a hospital, but onto a mountain road in the middle of nowhere. Throughout the Japanese war and the civil war that followed, this army was beaten continuously because it had no soul.

('China Shakes the World', J. Belden, 1949)

59

SOURCE 4

Red Army guerrilla unit of the 8th Route Army.

SOURCE 6 — Mao Zedong's explanation of Red Army guerrilla tactics

When the enemy advances, we retreat.
When the enemy camps, we harass.
When the enemy tires, we attack.
When the enemy retreats, we pursue.

SOURCE 7 — Resources

At that time (1946) opposition to Chiang Kai-shek did seem suicidal. The General had an army four times that of the Red Army, with a correspondingly greater fire power in artillery, machine guns and rifles. Moreover, he had an air force, railways, gunboats and motor transport while the Reds had none; Chiang had a potent economy, held all the big cities and had the most powerful arsenals. Still more, Chiang held almost the entire sea coast, had access to foreign trade and was recognized by foreign powers. Unquestionably, Chiang had the superior-looking war machine.

('China Shakes the World', J. Belden, 1949)

SOURCE 5

The GMD on parade

SOURCE 8 — An account by a Red Guard

There were five brigades of us, and I was leader of one of them. But we had no weapons. So the village blacksmiths took the farm tools and made spears out of them; but there were not even enough of those to go around, so we made dummy ones. Each of us had three wooden hand grenades. Our uniform was a red armlet. At a distance we looked heavily armed. We found silver paper and used it to cover our wooden bayonets. They glinted in the sun. We frightened the landowners.

The women and children kept guard along the roads and outside the villages. We did not let anyone pass who did not have a permit from our revolutionary committee. Each brigade had a big red flag, and we carried these in front of us when we marched.

(from 'Report from a Chinese village', Myrdal, 1965)

2 — Attitudes to the peasants

SOURCE 1 — The peasants as the leaders of the revolution

This great mass of poor peasants are the backbone of the peasant associations, the vanguard in the overthrow of the enemy, and the heroes who have performed the great revolutionary task which for long years was left undone. Leadership by the poor peasants is absolutely necessary. Without the poor peasants there would be no revolution. To deny their role is to deny the revolution. To attack them is to attack the revolution.

(Mao Zedong, 'Selected Works', 1927)

SOURCE 2 — An interview with a Red Army commander

In 1928 my forces in Hunan had dwindled to a little over two thousand men. We were surrounded. The GMD troops burned down all the houses in the area, seized all the food and blockaded us. We had no cloth, we used bark to make short tunics, and we cut up the legs of our trousers to make shoes. Our hair grew long, we had no shelter, no lights, no salt. We were sick and half starved. The peasants were no better off, and we would not touch what little they had.

But the peasants encouraged us. They dug up the grain they had hidden from the GMD troops and gave it to us, and they ate potatoes and wild roots. They hated the GMD for burning their homes and stealing their food. Even before we arrived they had fought the landlords and tax-collectors, so they welcomed us. Many joined us, and nearly all helped us in some way. They wanted us to win! And because of that we fought on and broke the blockade.

('Red Star Over China', Edgar Snow, 1937)

SOURCE 3

Peasants helping Red Army troops sabotage transport in the war against Japan. Why do you think this photograph was taken?

SOURCE 4 — Red Army rules

Obey the following forms of conduct:
1 Speak politely.
2 Pay fairly for what you buy.
3 Return everything you borrow.
4 Pay for anything you damage.
5 Do not hit or swear at people.
6 Do not damage crops.
7 Do not take liberties with women.
8 Do not ill-treat captives.

SOURCE 5

Village women making uniforms and bandages for the Red Army.

SOURCE 6

Children were sometimes used as lookouts and messengers for the Red Army.

3 — Attitudes to the Japanese Occupation

SOURCE 1

The Japanese did not have enough soldiers to occupy all villages so they launched the "Three-All Policy" — Kill All, Burn All, Loot All. This was a village in North China after a swift Japanese raid.

SOURCE 2 — A communist official describes the effect of the Japanese occupation

Whenever we have enough organisers to explain the situation, it is easy to get the people on our side. Even guerrilla forces armed by the Japanese often desert to us with their new equipment. The savagery of the Japanese is our best argument.

They massacred the entire population of seven villages, accusing them all of being Soviet agents. Throughout Northern Shaanxi they burn nearly half the houses in the places they occupy. They are exceptionally brutal towards any local villagers who try to protect their women.

Shortly after this, our army came into the territory, held a great mass meeting on the site of one of the burned villages, and recruited from surrounding villages a force of several thousand farmers to fight the Japanese.

SOURCE 3 — A Japanese view

In recent years practically no serious fighting has taken place on the GMD front, the sword of the Japanese army being chiefly pointed at the communist areas. The ruling group in the GMD has carried out a passive policy against Japan while opposing the people within its own country.

(from 'Asahi Shinbun', a Tokyo newspaper, 1944)

SOURCE 4 — The USA's view

The Chinese will to fight Japan had vanished. The main GMD effort was concentrated on containing the communists in the north and on their own political squabbles.

(from US Department of State Report)

4 — Leadership

SOURCE 1 — The leaders

Mao Zedong

Very few people in 1935, perhaps not even Mao Zedong himself, believed that one day he would rule China. He never **looked** a future ruler of China. He was casual about his clothes. One hot day in 1937 he shocked a Western observer by taking off his trousers and continuing his discussions with his generals in his pants.

Yet as time went by his reputation grew. A meeting with Mao might have a real effect on one of his followers. One, Yuan Xue-gai wrote: 'As I grasped the Chairman's hand in both of mine, a streak of warmth came up from them and spread all over my body, making my heart throb all the faster.'

Mao was a complex personality. He was a peasant leader, expert guerrilla fighter, learned scholar and poet. Most important, he had a clear idea of what he wanted. He was absolutely convinced that any communist revolution must be led by the peasants and that in the meantime they must be indoctrinated, organised, armed and trained to fight. The peasants formed 90% of China's population and they had serious grievances. How could they be ignored in the plans for the revolution!

Chiang Kai-shek

Chiang Kai-shek was full of contradictions. He relied on Western support, but he did not like Europeans. He claimed to be the defender of China's independence but he made little effort to drive the Japanese out of China. He gave great commercial advantages to Western businessmen, the very men he did not like. He was very proud. He told his friends that he was the descendant of Duke Wen, who had been the founder of the Zhou Dynasty of Emperors. He was in fact the son of a small landowner. He was intolerant of any opposition to him, and increasingly used murder as his final argument. Chiang Kai-shek's pride made him contemptuous of all of humble birth, the great majority of the Chinese. He rarely wrote about the peasants, but once he said of them: 'The task of the peasants is to provide us with information concerning the enemy, food, comforts and soldiers for our armies.'

(adapted from E. M. Roberts, 'Mao Zedong and the Communist Revolution', 1970)

Famine victims in Hunan province. Did these people support the CCP, or just oppose the GMD?

SOURCE 2 — Extracts from General Stilwell's diary. In 1942 he was sent by the USA as military adviser to Generalissimo Chiang Kai-shek.

21 March 1942: Chiang Kai-shek has been boss so long, has so many yes-men, he has the idea he's infallible on any subject. . . It is impossible for me to compete with the swarm of parasites and sycophants that surround him.

15 June: Chiang Kai-shek's ignorance and fatuous complacency are appalling, the little dummy.

4 March 1943: the Chinese Red Cross is a racket. Stealing and sale of medicine is rampant . . . Higher-ups in army steal soldiers' food.

(quoted in F. Greene, 'Curtain of Ignorance', 1965)

I judge the GMD and the CCP by what I saw.

GMD: Corruption, chaos, neglect, taxes, words and deeds. Hoarding, black market, trading with the enemy.

CCP: reduce taxes, rents, interest, raise production and standard of living. Participate in government. Practise what they preach.

(L. Chassin, 'The Communist Conquest of China', 1966)

Communist China — Change and Continuities

Introducing communism

On 1 October 1949 Mao proclaimed the People's Republic of China; it became one of the largest communist states in the world. His aim was to transform China into a communist society loosely based on the principles of the founder of communism, Karl Marx. Put simply, these principles were:

- there should be equality between people
- there should be no hierarchy or privileged class of people
- there should be no private ownership
- no one should make a profit
- there should be no inherited wealth
- all should work for the common good of everyone else and the state
- the state should control all economic, cultural and political life until a perfect state of communism developed

These principles were worked out for countries in Western Europe that were already industrialised. China was a peasant society, however, so Mao Zedong had to adapt these principles to suit China's culture and circumstances.

Swings of the pendulum

Through the years of Mao's rule every aspect of life in China moved towards communism and the achievement of these principles. Sometimes the movement was slow, at other times it was very dramatic. However, since Mao's death China has become less strictly communist. These diagrams show this movement towards and away from Marx's ideal of communism.

This section looks at four areas of Chinese life — life on the land, industrial conditions, politics and culture.

▶ *Have all these areas changed in the same ways?*
▶ *Have they followed the swings of the pendulum?*
▶ *When was there slow change and when dramatic, sudden change?*

The next section looks at China's relations with other countries.

▶ *Has China's foreign policy followed the swings of the pendulum?*

The following section looks at the influence of Mao Zedong.

▶ *Have Mao's works and ideas even after his death been the main causes of change in China?*

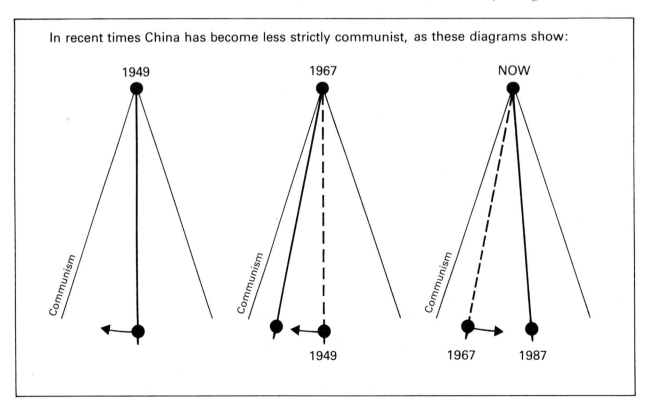

In recent times China has become less strictly communist, as these diagrams show:

The Revolution in China's Way of Life. Life on the Land

SOURCE 1 — A village revolution

The landlord, Schemer Jian, was glancing down from the stage, unwilling to admit defeat. For a moment he really was the master. He had been powerful for so long that it was difficult for anyone to dislodge him. The peasants had just been cursing him; but now he stood before them they faltered. . . The longer the silence lasted, the greater Jian's power became, until it looked as if he were going to win.

Then a man leapt out from the crowd. . . Rushing up to Schemer Jian he cursed him: 'You murderer! You trampled our village under your feet! You killed people for money. Today we're going to settle all old scores, and do a thorough job of it. Do you still want to frighten people? Kneel down! Kneel to all the villagers!' He pushed Jian hard, while the crowd echoed: 'Kneel down! Kneel down!'

The crowd shouted 'Make him wear the hat! Put on the hat!' A boy jumped up, lifted the hat and set it on Schemer Jian's head at the same time spitting at him and cursing. . .

Jian lowered his head completely. The tall paper hat made him look like a clown. Bent from the waist, he had lost all his power, had become the people's prisoner.

The man who had cursed Jian turned to face the crowd. It was Yong Zheng, the chairman of the peasants' association. 'Friends!' said Yong Zheng. 'Look at him and look at me! See how soft and

The trial of a landlord before a people's court in 1953. What can you tell from the picture about the attitudes of those involved?

delicate he is: it's not cold yet but he's wearing a lined gown. Then look at me, look at yourselves. Do we look like human beings? When our mothers bore us, we were all alike! We've poured our blood and sweat to feed him. He's been living on our blood and sweat, but today we want him to give back money for money, life for life, isn't that right?'

'Right! Give back money for money, life for life!'. . . 'All peasants are brothers!' 'Support Chairman Mao!' 'Follow Chairman Mao to the end!'

Peasants surged up onto the stage, shouting wildly: 'Kill him! A life for our lives!'

A group of villagers rushed to beat him. It was not clear who started, but one struck the first blow and others fought to get at him. One feeling animated them all — vengeance!

(adapted from Ding Ling, 'The Sun Shines over the Sankgkan River', 1948)

Mao believed that these trials, held soon after the CCP came to power in 1949, were 'necessary evils' and that they were the first step on the road to communism.

▶ *Why did he think they were necessary?*
▶ *Why were the landlords brought before <u>People's Courts</u>?*

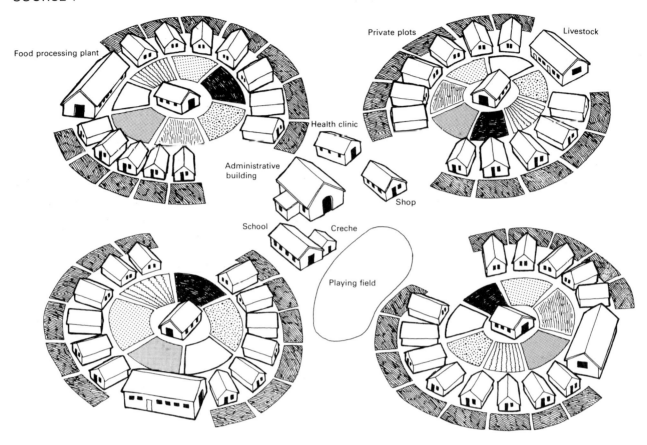

Food processing plant

Private plots

Livestock

Health clinic

Administrative building

Shop

School

Creche

Playing field

The layout of a typical commune. How does this layout support the ideals of a commune?

► *How have the peasants' lives changed?*

► *How haven't their lives changed?*

► *Read the following section on communes and then consider if Shen Fa-liang and Zhong-lai have exaggerated anything in this account.*

Communes for communism

In the late 1950s, under the Great Leap Forward, communes of hundreds of thousands of people were established around China. Mao hoped that commune life would soon lead to the ideal communist society. People would not own property themselves but everyone would work for the good of society as a whole. The diagram above shows a typical small rural commune of the early 1960s, when people were allowed small private plots to grow vegetables and keep livestock. At first, the plan was to hand over all land, and even possessions such as tools, furniture and saucepans, to the commune. However, by the early 1960s, people were allowed private plots to grow vegetables and keep livestock. During the Cultural Revolution these private plots were swept away and strict communist principles were applied again.

SOURCE 2 — Before and after

Two peasants from Langhow describe how their lives changed after Land Reform in 1952.

Shen Fa-liang, the former hired labourer, said 'Life is much better than before. Now I have land a house and work to do. There is food in my house. I work very hard but I enjoy the results of my work because I carry all the results of my work back home and put it in my own jars. In the past it was just the opposite. I worked very hard in all weather but all that work was for others. All the food went to someone else's pantry. Now I work for myself.'

Zhong-lai's wife felt the same way: 'In the old days I worked as a servant. I was busy every night until midnight, and I had to get up before dawn. Now I am very busy too but I work for myself. This is happy labour. . . My condition now is good. I've got a house, land to till, clothes to wear and the right to speak. Who dared speak before? In the past when I served in other families, I was often beaten or cursed. To live in one's own house and eat out of one's own bowl is the happiest life.'

(William Hinton, 'Fanshen', 1966)

"Learn from Dazhai"

In the mid-1960s the Dazhai commune in Shaanxi province was publicised as a model commune which all were encouraged to copy. It was in a remote and mountainous region which had alternate periods of drought, torrential rainfall and harsh winds. The 295 people of Dazhai all worked hard to build terraced fields and increase the grain yield from 0.75 to 7.5 tonnes per hectare. Eventually they bought tractors and trucks and built a school and new houses with electric light and piped water. According to their leaders their success was due to putting into practice the thoughts of Mao Zedong. However, in 1980 the 'People's Daily' confessed that Dazhai had not really relied on its own efforts to terrace rocky hills and dig irrigation ditches. They had received huge amounts of government money and even the help of the army to build a showpiece commune.

▶ *The Dazhai commune was a fraud. Does this mean that communism had failed in China?*
▶ *Consider how life on the land has altered from Land Reform in 1949 to the situation today.*
▶ *Read again the principles of communism outlined on page 64. At what point were they closest to being achieved? Were any of them broken at any time?*

SOURCE 4

A propaganda poster. The slogan says "In agriculture learn from Dazhai".

SOURCE 3 — The new responsibility system

When I first went there in 1972, during the Cultural Revolution, it was called the Xi Hu Tea Commune. Xi Hu had fallen into the hands of political activists, Maoists to the marrow. They emphasised how communal labour and equal wages had liberated the tea growers. Questions about production or quality were brushed aside. In the kindergarten children sang 'We are sailing the seas of life with Chairman Mao as our helmsman.'

By 1985 even pictures of the Great Helmsman had disappeared, together with the name Xi Hu Commune. It was now the Shuang Feng Tea Brigade. In 1978 families averaged 860 yuan (about £250) a year. By 1984 this had climbed to 2,700 yuan.

Shuang Feng's tea growers are not producing significantly more tea than there were three or four years ago. But the quality is much higher. In 1983 the 75 acres of tea were divided between 236 families. The more valuable small-leaf tea each family produces, the richer it gets.

'It's easy to understand,' says a local woman. 'Before the new system, when everyone made the same money no matter how hard or little they worked, it was easier to pick large leaves which made low-quality tea. But small-leaf tea sells for more. Now everyone wants to pick often, maybe 30 times a year, instead of six or seven. So the weight of the tea produced each year is about the same, but the quality is first class.'

People used to stand about waiting for the Party to tell them when to pick. Now each family decides.

(adapted from 'The Observer', 29 September 1985)

Industrial Life

The Great Leap Forward 1958

Mao wanted to involve all Chinese people in the Great Leap. He told people to 'work hard for three years, be happy for a thousand.' Especially important was the production of iron and steel, and peasants were encouraged to build makeshift furnaces in their backyards. They melted down radiators, pots, pans and any scrap they could find. There were stories in the papers that people worked day and night for weeks on end to produce iron for industry.

SOURCE 1

These pictures were published in "China Pictorial" in 1958 and "China Reconstructs" in 1973. Why would the Chinese government want to show pictures like these to the outside world? If they are propaganda, are they still of use to historians?

SOURCE 2

Heroes All

SOURCE 3 — Attitudes of the workers

On the railroad construction project everyone worked hard. All strove to be heroes and nobody lagged behind. People were enthusiastic.

We launched all sorts of competitions. There was a woman from Dianshi. She could haul 1000 catties of stone in a cart uphill or down. Men liked to work with her because she put all her strength into her work. She carried two big baskets on her carrying pole and no man could beat her.

(from 'Shenfan' by W. Hinton, 1983)

SOURCE 4

Production Figures (in million physical units)

	1952 (actual)	1957 (actual)	1959 (claim)	1964 (estimate)
Coal (tons)	66.5	130.7	347.8	209
Oil (tons)	0.4	1.5	3.7	8.4
Steel (tons)	1.3	5.3	13.3	9.5
Grain (tons)	154.5	185	270	180
Cotton (tons)	1.3	1.6	2.3	1.5

(1952, 1957, 1959 figures from Official Chinese Sources. 1964 estimate from the Yearbook of the Great Soviet Encyclopaedia, Moscow, 1965.)

▶ *How reliable are these figures?*
▶ *Although the Chinese authorities' claims about the production figures in 1959 were published, none were released in the following years. Why was this? What do the 1964 estimates indicate?*
▶ *Is the Yearbook of the Great Soviet Encyclopaedia reliable?*
▶ *How can the production figures for oil be explained?*
▶ *Do these figures indicate that the Great Leap Forward was a success or not?*

SOURCE 5

This cartoon, drawn in 1961, is typical of many which were printed in daily newspapers. What is the message behind it?

The Four Modernisations

In the late 1970s the Chinese leaders launched their new policy of the Four Modernisations, which aimed to update industry, agriculture, defence, science and technology. They needed outside expertise and assistance to do this, so the so-called 'Open Door' policy was begun. Chinese leaders sought help from Western governments and countries.

SOURCE 6 — Economic facts and figures, 1983

China's Foreign Trade
Imports   42,200m yuan
Exports   43,800m yuan (21 times their 1950 value)

Tourism
Earned 9.48m in 1983 (5 times the total in 1978)

Average per capita consumption
1952   76 yuan
1983   288 yuan (£100)

(from 'Beijing Review', 8th October 1984)

SOURCE 7 — Exports to China in 1984

	(Millions of US dollars)
Japan	6680
USA	2860
West Germany	1038
Canada	987
Australia	747
UK	432
Italy	380
France	312

SOURCE 8

All this has led to more contacts with the West through tourism, cultural exchange and sporting links. There has even been talk of opening hamburger shops on the Great Wall.

(from 'The Times', 8 February 1985)

SOURCE 9 — New business people

China's newspapers nowadays are filled with stories about 10,000 yuan a year (just over £3,000) businessmen who make about three times as much as Party General Secretary Hu Yaobang, one of the three men who run the country.

Gao Yutian is a former 'capitalist tail'. That is what the Party called him during the Cultural Revolution (1966–1976), when he suggested that skilled workers could make more money working on their own.

Ten-Thousand-Yuan Gao appeared wholly pleased with life. He has made his pile as a house and factory painter in Jiangsu province, one of the most prosperous in China, where everywhere peasants are putting up new houses. Mr Gao employs 20 painters, owns a van and a truck and, miraculously in China where such instruments are nearly unknown, possesses a private telephone. Two children's bedrooms: 'My children don't have to sleep in the same bed'. Dining and sitting rooms, kitchen with two-wok stove and fridge, and outside loo, just for the family. The workers use a second.

'We owe all this to Deng Xiaoping and Premier Zhao,' says Gao. 'Before them we were really stupid, feudal, all "eating out of the same pot". Now really intelligent people can do well.' He has clearly been reading Party statements on the economy.

(adapted from 'The Observer', 29 September 1985)

▶ *Consider what have been the main characteristics of China's industrial life since 1949. Add to this list – working together, increased production, ...*

▶ *In what ways has industrial life changed in recent years?*

Women electricians at the Fushun Electric Power Station. Stories of women successfully doing jobs previously done by men are common in Chinese magazines. Why?

Political Control

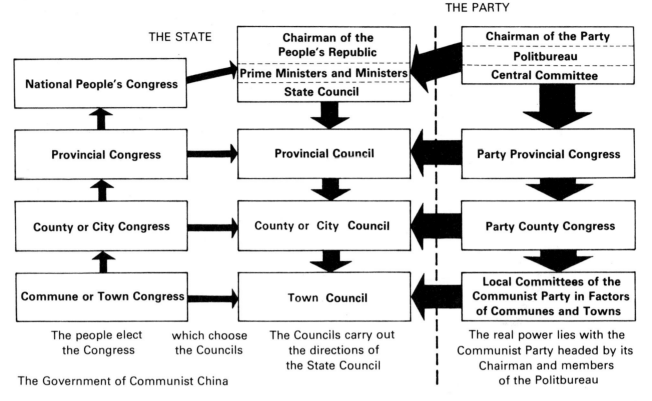

The Government of Communist China

The people elect the Congress — which choose the Councils — The Councils carry out the directions of the State Council — The real power lies with the Communist Party headed by its Chairman and members of the Politbureau

The structure of government in China. The width of the arrows shows the relative degree of power and influence.

SOURCE 1

The People's Republic of China is a Socialist State led by the working class. The working class exercises leadership over the State through the Communist Party of China. The State believes in democracy. The people have the right to take part in the management of State affairs and of all economic and cultural matters.

(adapted from the State Constitution, 1978)

Chinese communists interpret democracy in their own way. It is very different from our understanding of democracy. In Britain there is a government chosen in elections in which many political parties take part. There is also an independent legal system under which individual rights are protected. The Chinese communists consider their 'People's Democracy' is superior to this, for two reasons. Firstly, members of government are elected at all levels, and secondly, the Communist Party monopolises political power on behalf of the working class. The laws passed and decisions taken by government are supposed to be checked by the Party to see that working class interests are always protected.

In reality it is the Communist Party which has real power. It was the Party which began important policy decisions such as the Great Leap Forward, the struggle against the 'Gang of Four', and the 'Four Modernisations'. And, in 1977 there were only 38.5 million members of the Communist Party out of a population of 971 million (that is 4 per cent of the population).

▶ *The Chinese people seem to have more of a role in government today than ever they had under the GMD or the Manchu emperors, but does this seem to be a real involvement?*

Freedom

SOURCE 2

All citizens enjoy freedom of speech, correspondence, the press, assembly, association, procession and demonstration, and the freedom to strike, the right to speak out freely, hold great debates and write big-character posters. They also enjoy freedom to believe in religion and to spread atheism.

(The State Constitution, 1978)

In 1978 and 1979 there was an outburst of demands for more freedom. The Chinese tradition of expressing views in wall posters was used, and many appeared on the so-called 'Democracy Wall' near Beijing's bus depot. One such poster was written by Wei Jingsheng:

SOURCE 3 — Democracy

After the defeat of the 'Gang of Four' we began to dream of democracy and prosperity again, but our odious political system has not been amended in the slightest by Hua and Deng . . . the wearisome drivel of 'class struggle' has now been replaced with a new panacea — the 'Four Modernisations'.

According to Socialism, the masses hold all political power, but what rights and powers do we have for we must still obey the orders of the central authorities? If we wish to stop suffering from slavery and misery there is only one way — Democracy.

Genuine Democracy is a system which allows the people to dismiss and replace their representatives at any time and prevent them from abusing their powers. The difference between Democracy in China and in the Western countries is as night and day. In our country, if in a private conversation you express the slightest doubt concerning our great helmsman Mao Zedong, you immediately see in front of you the gaping gates of a jail.

We want to become the masters of our own destiny. We need no gods and no emperors . . . totalitarian Fascism can only bring us disaster; let us unite under the banner of Democracy.

As for those 'great leaders' who have swindled the people of their most precious rights for several decades, they may now all go to hell. The 'Democracy Wall' in Beijing has become the people's first fortress in the struggle against all reactionary forces whose worst examples this century are Nazi Germany, the Soviet Union and the 'New China'. Blood will be shed . . . but the reactionary forces will never again succeed in obliterating our Democracy flag in their poisonous mist.

(from a wall poster, 1979)

SOURCE 4 — Labour camps

What they are guarding is one of the 'Reform through Labour' camps for which this remote north-west province is famous.

The governor of Qinghai, Mr Huang Jingbo, admits that at least 10,000 people are undergoing 'labour reform' in his province. Independent sources suggest that the number of prisoners in Qinghai could be between 50,000 and 100,000.

These provinces in north-west China have been known almost since the founding of the People's Republic as the home of the Chinese gulags, to which 'counter-revolutionaries' and serious criminals are sent from all over the country. It is a far more severe sentence than to serve time nearer home in one of the regular municipal jails.'

(adapted from 'The Guardian', 19 August 1984)

▶ *Are the Chinese more or less free than under the Manchus?*

▶ *Are the terms of the 1978 State Constitution (Sources 1 and 2) being kept?*

SOURCE 5

This cartoon is a comment on government policy in China in 1987. The expression 'Let a thousand flowers blossom' is a parody of Mao's slogan of 1956, encouraging people to express their own opinions; even criticisms of the way China is run. The cartoonist's interpretation of the government's reaction to any 'blossoming' of news is represented by the lawn-mower.

LET A THOUSAND FLOWERS BLOSSOM...

Entertainment and Education

How has communism affected life in China? You would notice great differences between life in China and in Britain in entertainment and education.

▶ *What do these sources tell us about Chinese attitudes to entertainment and education and how they have changed since 1949?*

Entertainment

SOURCE 1

In 1979 I visited China and met several arts personalities, including several poets who had not written anything for up to 10 years. I remember talking with a frail, thin old man who walked with a stick. It turned out he was China's greatest film director. In fact, he was only 48 years old but he had spent six years in prison during the Cultural Revolution, and he had been beaten and had been badly injured. I later learned he died a couple of months later.

(from an interview with Arthur Miller, 'BBC Omnibus', 12 July 1985)

A photograph taken during Wham!'s tour of China. Was this photograph taken for use in China or Britain?

In April 1985 the British pop group Wham! toured China. This was the first time a Western pop group had played in China and was seen as an important breakthrough by the West. In China relatively few people knew of the tour, and even fewer knew (or cared) who Wham! were. The British press, however, made much of the tour and mocked the Chinese translations of the group's songs: for example, 'Careless Whisper' it was said translated as 'Speaking frankly without evil intent'.

SOURCE 2 — Wham! in China

More than 1000 Chinese people queued through the night for tickets for the first concert ever played behind the Bamboo Curtain by a major Western rock band.

Though tickets cost nearly £2 each — three days' wages for a manual worker — the fans were promised a free Wham! cassette with every ticket.

Later a lavish banquet was staged for the duo by the Chinese government.

The Communist Party is worried about the moral risk of allowing a Western pop group to play to the city's young people.

Just 12 months ago dancing was illegal in Beijing and discos were banned even in tourist hotels because they were 'decadent'.

Wham! will strike all sexual innuendos from their stage show, and they are expected to turn their sound system down to half volume.

(adapted from 'Daily Mirror' report, 6 April 1985)

SOURCE 3 — China's Hottest Jazz Band

The 36th floor of Nanjing's Jinling Hotel is the home of China's hottest jazz band, Jimmy King and his Aloha Hawaiians. Jimmy King and his band were famous before the revolution in 1949, but later Jimmy King was sent to teach English and then to a labour camp for political education. When he returned, it was politically daring of the hotel to hire Jimmy King, symbol of night-life before Communism. 'Those above' (the Party leaders) didn't like the idea, but three of the hotel managers are also Party members. They insisted that the Party puts productivity first, and Jimmy King means profits. That was enough. So every night the band play their old favourites — Perry Como, Bing Crosby, and their new singer's favourite British singer, Vera Lynn.

(adapted from 'The Observer', 29 September 1985)

Education

SOURCE 4 — A story for Chinese children aged four to six

I am on duty today,
Helping in our nursery.
I get up with the sunrise,
And go to work happily.

First Dongdong helps me move the table.
Then we arrange the chairs.
We tidy the bookshelf
And put the toys in order.

We stretch up high and bend down low.
'One, two; one, two; one, two.'
How well we keep together!
Exercising every day keeps us healthy.

I give out the pencils.
Dongdong passes round the paper.
We learn our numbers, then we write,
Listening carefully to our teacher.

Dongdong and I put out the little bowls
And we fill them with rice.
Wash your hands quickly, little friends.
It's a good habit to wash before eating.

After our nap we have refreshments.
Dongdong passes the sweets, I take round the biscuits.
The large and good ones I give to other children,
And keep the small ones for myself.

And now we tidy the tables and chairs,
And put away the books and toys:
All in order for tomorrow,
So our friends on duty will have no trouble.

(from 'I am on Duty Today' by Yang Yi and Liang Ge, which appears in a children's story book, written in 1966 and still used in 1981.)

▶ *Identify the attitudes that the story is striving to teach.*

SOURCE 5 — Educational aims

While their main task is to study, they should also learn other things, that is, industrial work, farming and military affairs. They should also criticise the bourgeoisie.

Education must serve proletarian politics and be combined with productive labour.

(Mao Zedong directive, 1966)

SOURCE 6

We must train workers with high attainment in science and culture if we are to master modern science, if we are to create higher productivity than under capitalism and transform China into a powerful modern Socialist country, and, what is more, ultimately defeat the bourgeoisie. These demands are in the interests of proletarian politics.

(Deng Xiaoping, 1978)

SOURCE 7 — A typical secondary school day in Beijing in the early 1970s

0800	A communist text
0810	Chinese language
0900	Mathematics
0950	Physical exercise followed by a break
1020	English
1115	Science
1200	Lunch
1400	Politics
1450	Music
1540	Newspaper reading
1600	PE/Sport
1830	School finishes

SOURCE 8 — Percentage of population illiterate

1949	85%
1952	40%
1965	25%

(official Chinese figures)

Women hold up half the sky

Equality

Attitudes to the role of women in China have changed. Officially women are equal to men, but there remain centuries of prejudice and inequality to break down.

▶ *Link up the following quotations with the people who wrote them:*

1 *Mao Zedong*
2 *Ancient Chinese philosopher, Mencius*
3 *The 'People's Daily' in November 1974 trying to encourage more modern attitudes*
4 *The memories of an old woman before the revolution.*

A Between husband and wife there should be attention to their separate functions — a husband should be responsible for everything outside the home and a wife should be responsible for everything inside the home.

B It was not considered proper for women to expose any part of the body except the face and hands. All we were allowed to do was a little bit of light work in the garden, if we had one. No matter what happened, drought or flood, we could not go out to help the menfolk save the crops!

C China's women are a vast reserve of labour power. The reserve should be tapped in the struggle to build a great socialist state.

D There is still the attitude that 'women go home to cook meals, feed the pigs and shut up chickens, while men go home to smoke their pipes and wait for food and drink.' Some even laugh at those male comrades who help their wives with housework.

SOURCE 1 — Chinese marriage laws

Article 1 The feudal marriage system is based on compulsory arrangements and the superiority of man over woman, and ignores the children's interests. It shall be abolished.

The new democratic marriage system is based on the free choice of partners, on monogamy, on equal rights for both sexes and on the protection of the lawful interests of woman and children. It shall be put into effect.

Article 2 Bigamy, child betrothal, interference with the remarriage of widows, and the exaction of money or gifts in connection with marriages, shall be prohibited.

Article 4 A marriage can be contracted only after the man has reached 20 years of age and the woman 18 years of age.

Article 7 Husband and wife are companions living together and shall enjoy equal status in the home.

Article 10 Both husband and wife shall have equal rights in the possession and management of family property.

Article 11 Both husband and wife shall have the right to use his or her own family name.

Article 13 Parents have the duty to rear and educate their children; the children have the duty to support and assist their parents. Infanticide by drowning and similar criminal acts are strictly prohibited.

(as issued by The People's Republic of China, 1 May 1950)

▶ *This law was the first to be passed by the People's Republic of China. What practical reasons would have made this so important?*

SOURCE 2

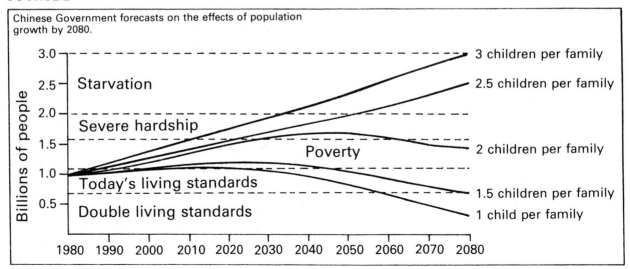

Chinese Government forecasts on the effects of population growth by 2080.

- 3 children per family
- 2.5 children per family
- 2 children per family
- 1.5 children per family
- 1 child per family

Starvation
Severe hardship
Poverty
Today's living standards
Double living standards

Billions of people

1980 1990 2000 2010 2020 2030 2040 2050 2060 2070 2080

SOURCE 3

A government poster supporting the idea that "one child is enough". Why is this one child policy so important for China's future? What problems is it likely to face?

Women now take a full part in political activity. However, in 1977 only 39 of the 147 elected members of the Standing Committee of the National People's Congress and only two of the 20 ministers were women.

▶ *Does this mean that equality has not been achieved in China?*

Population control

Between 1949 and 1980 the population of China doubled, and the authorities fear that if the population continues to increase it will result in mass starvation in the next century. On 1 January 1979 the policy of allowing only one child per family was introduced. When a couple want to marry they have to obtain permission from their local family-planning officer. Before they marry they have to take a written test in family planning and they must obtain permission before they have a child.

By 1984 the government appeared to be relaxing its one-child policy. Some were claiming that spoilt single children were *xia huangdi* or 'little emperors'. The policy was clearly working, as in 1984 the population growth rate fell to 10 per 1000 — the lowest rate since the republic was founded in 1949. This relaxation allows some specified categories of parents to have two children. Although only a minor concession it is certainly a step away from the time when it was declared that 'giving birth to children is not just a family affair.'

SOURCE 4 — Stop the slaughter of baby girls

Chinese peasants are allowing their baby girls to die at such a rate that a call has gone out to save them. Nothing but murder or deliberate neglect can explain why in some communes just 200 girls survive out of every 500 children born.

These figures, reported in 'China Youth Daily', highlight the reappearance of female infanticide, usually by abandonment or exposure but sometimes by drowning. It is another of China's traditional practices, such as prostitution and arranged marriage, once claimed to have disappeared under communism.

The rise in the killing of girls is a direct result of China's one-child family drive, which seeks dramatically to reduce the population of more than one billion. But an extensive birth-control campaign has not prevented a rise in population.

At a local level, rewards and punishments are being used to persuade newly-weds to limit themselves to one child.

Many Chinese still believe that without a son there can be no descendants. Only male children hand down the family name and can worship and nourish their ancestors.

(adapted from 'The Observer', 12 December 1982)

SOURCE 5 — Revolving around the sun?

China and the Superpowers

China's strategic position in the world.

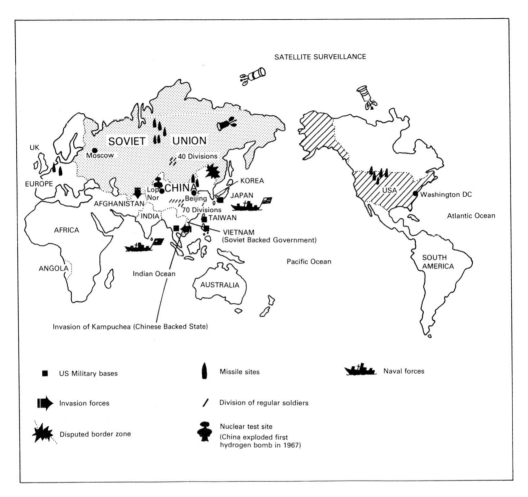

SATELLITE SURVEILLANCE

UK
EUROPE
SOVIET UNION
Moscow
40 Divisions
KOREA
Lop Nor
CHINA
Beijing
JAPAN
AFGHANISTAN
70 Divisions
TAIWAN
INDIA
VIETNAM
(Soviet Backed Government)
AFRICA
ANGOLA
Indian Ocean
Invasion of Kampuchea (Chinese Backed State)
AUSTRALIA
Pacific Ocean
USA
Washington DC
Atlantic Ocean
SOUTH
AMERICA

■ US Military bases

Missile sites

Naval forces

Invasion forces

/ Division of regular soldiers

Disputed border zone

Nuclear test site
(China exploded first
hydrogen bomb in 1967)

▶ *What would you expect was China's attitude to:*

1 *The British Conservative Party winning the 1979 General Election?*
2 *American requests for trade deals?*
3 *The Soviet space programme?*
4 *The Strategic Arms Limitation Talks between America and the Soviet Union in the early 1970s?*
5 *Soviet aid to the communist forces fighting for independence in Angola?*

China's attitude might appear surprising. Despite being the largest communist country, based on the principles of Marxism, China took an apparently contradictory view of these events and personalities. The Chinese leadership welcomed the British Conservative victory and the American trade deals, but were critical of the SALT negotiations and the Soviet aid given to the Angolan freedom fighters, and were worried by the military implications of the Soviet space programme.

These attitudes can be explained firstly by her fear of the power of the Soviet Union. Although the USSR is a fellow communist country, there has been considerable suspicion and tension between them. Secondly, China's internal condition has led to her seeking friends and technical assistance from Western countries.

There are three key questions to be investigated in understanding China's current foreign relations:

1 Why are Sino-Soviet relations so strained?
2 Why are Sino-American relations so good?
3 What is China's place in the world?

In order to understand these questions, we need to investigate how China's foreign relations have developed since 1949. There have been many twists and turns in her relations.

▶ *By referring to the time chart in the narrative on page 31, place the following sources in chronological order and explain what each tells us.*

76

SOURCE 1

Russian poster in praise of Chinese people. 'Glory to the great Chinese people who have gained freedom, independence and happiness'.

SOURCE 2

It was announced today that the Chinese Olympic Committee will now not send a team of athletes to the Moscow Olympic Games. This decision by the Chinese authorities is in response to the call by the US government to boycott the Moscow Games following the Russian invasion of Afghanistan last winter.

(from a Radio News broadcast, 1980)

SOURCE 3

The delegation from the People's Republic of China taking their seats for the first time at the UN.

SOURCE 4

Spectacular provocations have been taking place amongst the border guards along the Amur-Ussuri River. On several occasions the Chinese have marched prisoners to the island in the centre of the river, accused them of being Soviet spies, and then beheaded them. Another favourite habit was forming up on the river ice, sticking out their tongues at the Soviet troops, then turning round and dropping their trousers in an ancient gesture of contempt.

(a description by a British journalist of the events along the Sino-Soviet border in 1969)

SOURCE 5

"Testing the Water", a cartoon drawn at the time of President Nixon's visit to Beijing. This was a dramatic step as it was the first visit by a Western leader to Communist China.

SOURCE 6

A new upsurge in the struggle against US imperialism is now growing throughout the world. Ever since World War II, US imperialism and its followers have been continuously launching wars of aggression and the people in various countries have been continuously fighting revolutionary wars to defeat the aggressors. People of the World, unite and defeat the US aggressors and all their running dogs!

(extract from a speech by Mao Zedong reported in 'China Reconstructs')

SOURCE 7

The Treaty of Friendship between ourselves and the USSR will be everlasting and can never be destroyed.

(Mao Zedong)

Sino-American Relations

In the Cold War years of the 1950s China regarded America as the arch-enemy. America had been an ally of the GMD and continued to support Chiang Kai-shek's government on Taiwan as the legitimate government of China, sending it thousands of dollars of economic and military aid. America organised resistance to the People's Republic of China's application to join the UNO. America imposed a strict embargo on all trade with China. The Chinese saw further evidence of America's anti-communist activities when US combat troops were sent to help fight in the Korean War (1950–1953) and in the Vietnam War (1965–1975). In both wars the USA fought alongside the governments of South Korea and South Vietnam to resist the invasion of communist forces from North Korea and North Vietnam. China saw both wars as a threat to its security, and sent aid to its fellow-communist governments.

▶ *Why did America get involved in the Korean War?*

SOURCE 1 — Korean War: killed and wounded

South Korea: 300,000 soldiers.
United Nations: (including US troops) 142,000 soldiers.
Chinese and North Korean: 150,000 soldiers.
Korean civilians: 1,000,000.

(based on United Nations estimates)

SOURCE 4

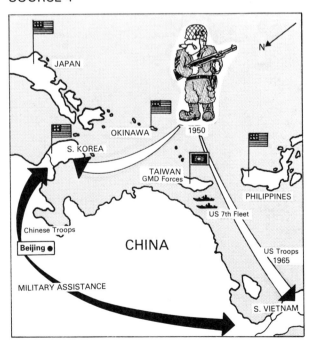

China's view of the USA's involvement in the Korean and Vietnam wars. Why did China feel threatened?

SOURCE 2

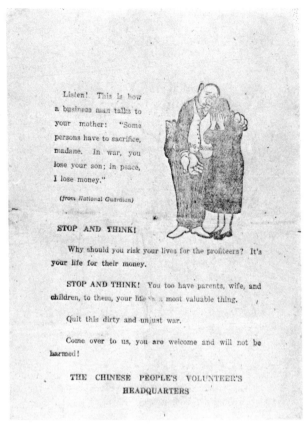

A Chinese propaganda leaflet dropped on US troops during the Vietnam war. Is this of use to historians even though it is propaganda?

SOURCE 3 — A Chinese children's song

There is an evil spirit:
His name is Johnson.
His mouth is all sweetness,
But he has a wolf's heart.
He bombs Vietnam cities
And hates the people.
Chinese and Vietnamese are all one family:
We will certainly not agree to this!
I wear a red scarf and join the demonstrations with Daddy.
With small throat but large voice I shout:
'US pirates get out, get out, get out'.

(quoted in 'China', L. Mitchinson, 1966)

SOURCE 5

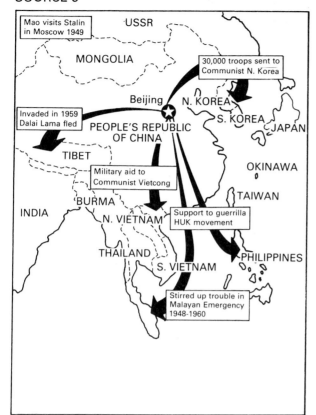

The USA's view of the dangerous influence of China. What might the USA be afraid of?

The Domino Theory. If one country falls to Communism, the others will follow!

SOURCE 7

'Look, buster, this is leap year — and you're chosen!'

This cartoon graphically shows the United States change of policy towards the Nationalist Chinese in Taiwan. What incidents between 1971 and 1974 best illustrate this change?

SOURCE 6 — The US position on China

On the Chinese mainland 600 million people are ruled by the Chinese Communist Party. That party came to power by violence, and, so far, has lived by violence. It retains power not by the will of the Chinese people but by massive, forcible repression. It fought the United Nations in Korea; it supported the Communist War in Indo-China; it took Tibet by force. It fomented the communist Huk rebellion in the Philippines and the communist insurrection in Malaya. It does not disguise its expansionist ambitions. It is bitterly hateful of the United States, which it considers a principal obstacle in the way of its path of conquest. As regards China, we have abstained from any act to encourage the communist regime — morally, politically or materially. Thus: We have not extended diplomatic recognition to the Chinese communist regime. We have opposed seating in the United Nations. We have not traded with communist China or sanctioned cultural exchanges with it.

(US Department of State Bulletin, 15 July 1953)

▶ *Consider the reasons why the United States was so against Communist China at this time.*

SOURCE 8 — Changing US policy

China exemplified the great changes that had occurred in the communist world. For years, our guiding principle was containment of what we considered a monolithic challenge. In the 1960s the forces of nationalism dissolved communist unity into divergent centres of power and doctrine, and our foreign policy began to differentiate among the communist capitals. But this process could not be truly effective as long as we were cut off from one-quarter of the globe's people. China in turn was emerging from its isolation and might be more receptive to overtures from foreign countries . . . We would deal with countries on the basis of their actions, not abstract ideological formulas. [The US and China] seemed to have no fundamental interests that need collide in the eager sweep of history.

(extract from President Nixon's Foreign Policy report to Congress, 1973)

▶ *Explain how American policy towards China has changed from 1953 to 1973.*
▶ *What might have brought about this change?*

Sino-Soviet Relations

SOURCE 1

'Krushchev, the despicable renegade to the Soviet people is in the company of US imperialist, chieftain Kennedy'.

This photograph and caption appeared in the Chinese magazine "China Reconstructs". Why is the caption so critical of Krushchev who followed Stalin as Russian leader?

Since the early days of the Chinese Communist Party the Soviet Union had given Chinese communities advice and assistance. However, the two countries were very different. In 1950 the Soviet Union was a powerful industrialised superpower, while China was still essentially a poor country with a peasant economy. It was not surprising that each had developed its own brand of communism and that they were taking different roads towards the socialist ideal. However, in the early days of the People's Republic, China was eager to seek friends; and the Soviet Union, in the midst of the Cold War with America, likewise sought friendship with this new fellow-communist state. In February 1950 Mao Zedong made a state visit to Moscow and signed a Treaty of Friendship with the USSR.

SOURCE 2 — A Treaty of Friendship

Vyshinski, Soviet Foreign Minister

The Treaty of Friendship . . . based on respect for the principle of equality, state independence and national sovereignty, seals the historic bonds between the peoples of the Soviet Union and China.

Mao Zedong

People can see that the unity of the two peoples of China and the Soviet Union, already solidified through a treaty, will be everlasting, unbreakable and inseparable by any people. This kind of unity not only will affect the prosperity of China and the Soviet Union but will certainly affect the future of humanity and the victory of world peace and justice.

(statements following the signing of the Sino-Soviet Treaty of Friendship, 1950)

▶ Why should historians be cautious in accepting public declarations such as this as reliable evidence of a country's feelings?
▶ List the reasons each side had for signing this treaty. (Consider economic and strategic reasons.)

These public utterances perhaps cover up Mao's true feelings. Mao insisted that the Soviet Union should not dominate the Chinese revolution and as he put it once himself: 'If the Russians break wind, we don't have to pretend it smells nice.'

80

SOURCE 3 — A letter from the Chinese to the Soviet Government

For several years there have been differences within the international communist movement. The central issue is whether or not to accept the fact that the people still living under the imperialist and capitalist system need to make revolution. It is wrong to believe that the contradiction between the proletariat and the bourgeoisie can be resolved without a proletarian revolution in every country and that the contradiction between the oppressed nations and imperialism can be resolved without revolution.

(quoted in 'KCA', 10-17 August 1963)

Khrushchev's explanation for the souring of relations after 1954 was different.

SOURCE 4 — The Soviet view

Ever since I first met Mao, I've known that Mao would never be able to reconcile himself to any other communist party being in any way superior to his own within the world communist movement. I remember that when I came back from China in 1954 I told my comrades, 'Conflict with China is inevitable'. I came to this conclusion on the basis of various remarks Mao had made. He's a nationalist, and at least when I knew him, he was bursting with an impatient desire to rule the world. His plan was to rule first China, then Asia, then . . . what?

(adapted from 'Khrushchev Remembers', N. Khrushchev, 1970)

These are the official explanations for the worsening of relations. However, some historians see more practical reasons, such as:

1   The Soviet Union refused to honour an agreement with China which had promised her help in building atomic weapons.
2   The Soviet Union refused to back China's claims for border areas in India and her claim to Taiwan.
3   The centuries-old disputes between the two countries over border territory.

▶ *Can you think of any other reasons?*
▶ *Can you detect any underlying reason beneath all these stated factors?*

SOURCE 5 — Chinese account of the 1969 border incident

The Soviet side sent two helicopters, dozens of tanks and armoured vehicles, and several hundred armed troops to intrude into the border area . . . They penetrated a depth of two kilometres, unwarrantedly fired at the Chinese frontier guards on normal patrol duty, killing and wounding many of them on the spot, and closed in on them. Driven beyond the limits of forbearance, the Chinese frontier guards were compelled to fight back in self-defence.

(from 'KCA', 1-8 November, 1969)

SOURCE 6 — Border clash!

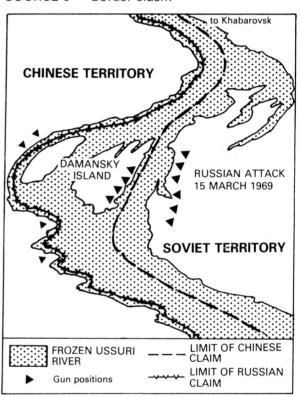

Border clash on the Ussuri River. Damansky Island is the Russian name for the disputed island. The Chinese call it Chenpoo.

SOURCE 7 — Russian account of the incident

The armed provocation staged by the Chinese authorities on the Soviet-Chinese border was planned in advance. On the previous day, 12 August, Soviet frontier guards observed that Army units were being moved up on the Chinese side of this section of the frontier, that there were intensive troop movements, and that communication lines were being put up. To avert a worsening of the situation the Soviet frontier authorities called on the frontier guards of the People's Republic of China to send a representative for talks. The latter declined . . .

(from 'KCA', 1-8 November, 1969)

Recent Developments

SOURCE 1 — China welcomes Kremlin in from the cold

Friday's arrival of a Soviet deputy prime minister, Ivan Arkhipov, represents an important diplomatic breakthrough.

Relations between the Russians and the Chinese are still frosty, but there are signs of a thaw for the first time since the Sino-Soviet dispute hardened in the early 1960s. Chinese and Russian border guards now eat and play cards together and watch each other's films. On the diplomatic front, Arkhipov's visit at the head of a trade mission is the highest-level contact between the Soviet Union and China since 1969.

At the heart of the political problem are what the Chinese describe as the 'three obstacles' — the strength of Soviet troops on the China border, Soviet support for the Vietnamese occupation of Kampuchea, and the Soviet occupation of Afghanistan. These issues must be settled, the Chinese insist, before they can improve political relations with Moscow.

The two sides are also still at odds over several territorial questions, including the ownership of islands in the Ussuri river and Chinese claims to lands forcibly ceded to Tsarist Russia in the nineteenth century.

In spite of the political problems, both sides have much to gain from economic dealings. The Soviet Union needs Chinese food and consumer goods.

For the Russians, a reduction in tension could allow them to divert military resources away from the Chinese frontier. Equally, the Chinese, who are preoccupied with a radical change in internal economic policy, have put the modernisation of the armed forces and defence expenditure at the bottom of the list.

(from 'The Sunday Times', 23 December 1984)

China, the USSR and the USA — changing relationships since 1949. What kind of diagram would you draw to show their relationship today?

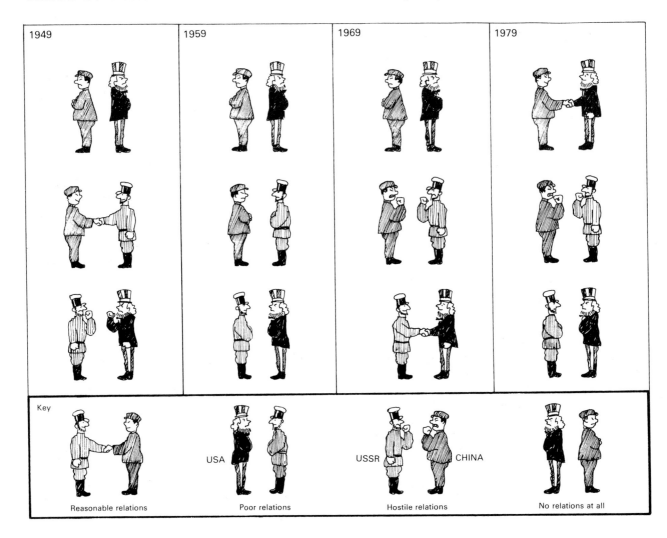

1949	1959	1969	1979

Key — Reasonable relations / Poor relations / Hostile relations / No relations at all

USA   USSR   CHINA

▶ *What obstacles to improved Sino-Soviet relations are mentioned in Source 1?*

▶ *What surprising military consequence is hinted at if Sino-Soviet relations improve?*

▶ *Who do you think would benefit most from improved relations – China or Russia? Give your reasons.*

▶ *How do you account for the changes in China's foreign relations with the Superpowers?*

In answering this last complex question one must not lose sight of the following:

1   Domestic and economic affairs frequently affect foreign relations.
2   Traditional nationalistic policies and geographical position influence attitudes to world developments.
3   Much diplomatic activity is secret, and official diplomatic declarations of views are not always clear and reliable statements of true feelings.

Traditional Chinese Foreign Policy Aims

SOURCE 2 — Traditional foreign policy

Until the nineteenth century China regarded herself as the 'centre of the world'. Isolated from the rest of the world, she was surrounded by lesser states who recognised Chinese supremacy. By 1900 China had not only lost her influence over neighbouring countries but was herself the subject of colonial exploitation. The hatred of foreign domination bred a strong sense of nationalism in China of all political views. Indeed it was the CCP's firm nationalist stand in the war against Japan that led many to support the communist cause. These historical factors have had an important bearing on Chinese thinking about foreign policy, which since 1949 has had two main purposes: the desire not to be dominated or humiliated by any other foreign power, and an obsessive concern with the security of Chinese borders.

(from 'China: Portrait of a Superpower', Long and Oates, 1981)

SOURCE 3 — Changing foreign policy

Without modern science and technology it is impossible to build modern agriculture, modern industry or modern national defence. To raise China's scientific and technological level we must rely on our own efforts. But independence does not mean shutting the door to the world, nor does self-reliance mean blind opposition to everything foreign. Any nation or country must learn from the strong points of other nations and countries, from their advanced science and technology.

(extract from a speech by Deputy Premier Deng quoted in 'KCA', 8 September 1978)

SOURCE 4

This cartoon was published when President Reagan visited China in 1984. What does it suggest was the reason for improved US-China relations?

SOURCE 5 — Deng Xiaoping's speech to the UN, 1975

Judging from the changes in international relations, the world today actually consists of three parts, or three worlds, that are both interconnected and in contradiction to one another. The United States and the Soviet Union make up the First World. The developing countries in Asia, Africa, Latin America and other regions make up the Third World. The developed countries between the two make up the Second World.

China is a Socialist country, and a developing country as well. China belongs to the Third World. China is not a Superpower, nor will she ever seek to be one. What is a Superpower? A Superpower is an imperialist country which everywhere subjects other countries to its aggression, interference, control, subversion or plunder and strives for world domination. If one day China should change her colour and turn into a Superpower, if she too should play the tyrant in the world, the people of the world should identify her social-imperialism, expose it, oppose it and work together with the Chinese people to overthrow it.

(printed in Beijing Review'. 19 April 1975)

▶ *What evidence could Deng give for claiming that the two Superpowers have been aggressive?*

▶ *Is the theme in Source 3 reminiscent of statements made at the time of the 1911 revolution?*

Mao — One man and his country

Outline of Time Chart

1893	Mao born
1911	Revolution
1918	Mao moved to Beijing
1921	Mao joined the CCP
1927-28	Organised Autumn Harvest Risings of peasants
1935	Elected leader of the CCP
1949	Declaration of the People's Republic of China
1950	Land Reform started
1956	100 Flowers Campaign
1958	Great Leap Forward started
1966	Cultural Revolution started
1976	Death of Mao

SOURCE 1 — In praise of Mao

To sail the seas
You need a helmsman.
Life and growth are dependent on sun.
Rain and dew
Nourish the crops.
To make a revolution
You need Mao Zedong.
Fish can't live without water
And a melon needs roots
The revolutionary masses
Need the Communist Party.
Mao Zedong's thought
Is the sun ever shining.

(from 'The Song of the Helmsman')

▶ Mao was called 'The Great Helmsman' — what evidence does this poem give us about how Chinese people thought about Mao?

▶ Opposite is a timeline showing the major events in Mao's life. You'll have read about these events earlier in this book. From this reading do you think the title 'The Great Helmsman' is justified?

Who was Mao Zedong?

SOURCE 2 — Part-tiger, part-monkey

Mid-parted black hair over a calm face, delicate hands, a gaze that bored into its target. Mole on the chin which was almost a relief from the broad pale face with no wrinkles.

Self-contained. Giving the impression of thinking of six things at once. Mao never lost the duality of being a taut wire of pure mind, yet also sensual as a cat.

Earthy enough to startle a visitor by reaching into his baggy trousers to deal with lice. He was a lumbering type of man.

The balance of his being came from a clash of opposites. He was part tiger, he said of himself, and part monkey. His handwriting suggests a man who chose his moods and bothered little about rules.

(adapted from 'Mao' by C. Terrill, 1980)

SOURCE 3 — In the hour of the Green Dragon

According to Chinese astrology Mao Zedong was born in the year of the Black Snake, in the hour of the Green Dragon, sign of a life destined for blood and violence and great victories alternating with humiliating compromises.

(from 'Mao for Beginners' Rius and friends, 1980)

SOURCE 4

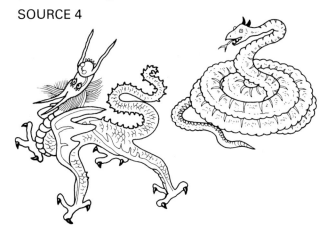

Mao's astrological birth signs. Did Mao's career follow their predictions?

What motivated Mao?

▶ *Why did Mao devote his life to politics and revolution? Was there one reason or many?*

SOURCE 5 — Rebels were ordinary people

Mao was born in Hunan, which was considered a rebellious area. When he was at school Mao saw the heads of peasant rebels stuck on the city gates as a warning. They had been the leaders of a group of starving peasants who had wanted food. Later Mao said 'This incident was discussed in my school for many days. It made a deep impression on me. Most of the other students sympathised with the rebels, but only from an observer's point of view. They did not understand that it had any relation to their own lives. They were merely interested in it as an exciting incident. I never forgot it. I felt that there with the rebels were ordinary people like my own family and I deeply resented the injustice of the treatment given to them.'

(adapted from 'Red Star over China', E. Snow)

SOURCE 6

SOURCE 7 — Mao's family

Mao's family may also have influenced him. Mao's father arranged his son's marriage and forced him to leave school to work. Mao said: 'There were two parties in the family. One was my father, the Ruling Power. The Opposition was made up of myself, my mother, my brother.'

SOURCE 8

SOURCE 9 — Our golden age lies ahead

Our Chinese people possess great energy. The greater the oppression, the greater their resistance. This energy must burst forth quickly. Our golden age, our age of brilliance and splendour lies ahead.

(Mao writing c. 1918, quoted in 'Mao for Beginners', Rius and friends, 1980)

SOURCE 10 — An act of violence

A revolution is not a dinner party, or writing an essay, or painting a picture, or doing embroidery. It cannot be so refined, so leisurely and gentle, so temperate, kind, courteous and restrained. A revolution is an act of violence, by which one class overthrows another.

(from 'The Selected Works of Mao Zedong', 1927)

SOURCE 11

How do the photographs on this page show Mao's changing role in China?

The cult of Maoism

Throughout the 1960s Mao Zedong developed a cult-style of leadership. He inspired the Chinese people and they turned to him for guidance in nearly all matters. The Chinese propaganda machine encouraged people to see him as a god-like figure — as George Orwell's "Big Borther". He provided China with an intellectual and cultural basis.

▶ *Can we be sure that all Chinese people accepted this kind of leadership?*
▶ *Many of these sources can be classed as propaganda – does that mean they are of no use to historians studying the period?*

SOURCE 1 — A poem by Mao, written in 1959 after he had paid his first return visit to his dead parents' home for 32 years

Like a dim dream recalled, I curse the long-fled past —
My native soil two and thirty years gone by.
The red flag round the serf, halberd in hand,
While the despot's black talons held his whip aloft.

Bitter sacrifices strengthen bold resolve
Which dares to make sun and moon shine in new skies.
Happy, I see wave upon wave of paddy and beans,
And all around heroes homebound in the evening mist.

(taken from J. C. Rush, 'A scrutable Mao', 1971)

SOURCE 2 — The Fable of the Foolish Old Man

An old man lived in northern China and was known as the Foolish Old Man of North Mountain. His house faced south and beyond his doorway stood two great peaks, obstructing his way. He called his sons and they began to dig up these mountains with determination. Another greybeard, known as the Wise Old Man, said 'How silly of you! It is impossible for you to dig up these mountains.' The Foolish Old Man replied, 'When I die my sons will carry on; when they die, there will be my grandsons and then their sons and grandsons, and so on. High as they are, the mountains can't grow any higher and every bit we dig they will be that much lower.' Having refused the Wise Old Man, he went on digging every day, unshaken in his conviction. God was moved by this and he sent down two angels who carried the mountains away on their backs.

This is an ancient Chinese story from the fourth century BC. Mao rewrote it during the Great Leap Forward. It was widely used in schools. Mao said the mountains represented imperialism and feudalism.

▶ *What is the message behind it?*

SOURCE 3 — Loyalty to Chairman Mao

Every day our teacher teaches us quotations and writings of Chairman Mao and his latest instructions concerning the Cultural Revolution.

During the New Year's holiday, when I was home from the kindergarten, Papa led a family meeting to 'fight self, repudiate revisionism'. During the meeting I remembered how every morning and evening our kindergarten teacher led us before Chairman Mao's portrait where we would pay our respects to Chairman Mao and wish him a long, long life. But we didn't do it at home. I wanted to be completely loyal to Chairman Mao so I said, 'Papa, we don't stand before Chairman Mao's portrait to pay our respects to him.' Papa, Mama and Grandma agreed with my idea. Papa said my idea was good and we would do it from then on.

(by Huang Ching — a six year old boy and quoted in 'China Reconstructs', June 1968)

SOURCE 4 — TRUTH

What I call belief means believing in Mao Zedong's thought; moreover, this belief must be steadfast and immovable. It is the symbol of truth. We must follow Chairman Mao steadfastly and eternally forward, following 100% and without the slightest reservation.

SOURCE 5 — The only clean people in the world

I began life as a student and at school acquired the ways of a student. I felt it was undignified to do even a little manual labour, such as carrying my own luggage in the presence of my fellow students. They were incapable of carrying anything, either on their shoulders or in their hands. At that time I felt that intellectuals were the only clean people in the world, while workers and peasants were dirty. But after I became a revolutionary and lived with workers and peasants and with soldiers I completely changed these early feelings. I came to feel that compared with the workers and peasants the unremoulded intellectuals were not clean, and that the workers and peasants were the cleanest people, and even though their hands were soiled and their feet smeared with cow-dung, they were really cleaner than the bourgeois intellectuals.

(extract from 'The Yanan Forum on Literature and Art', Mao Zedong)

SOURCE 6

Kindergarten children perform a song and dance show called "The Long March".

SOURCE 7

Mao reviewing Red Guards.

SOURCE 8

Mao, the father figure.

SOURCE 9

Red Guards with Mao's "Little Red Book" in a mass demonstration in Beijing.

The impact of Mao Zedong

SOURCE 1 — A miracle of surgery

Discussing the operation beforehand with a model of the tumour.

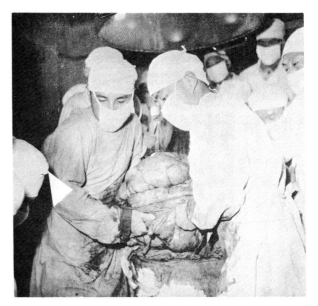

During surgery.

On 21 February this year a railway worker, Zui Bingwu, brought his wife in a cart to the health section of the People's Liberation Army in Beijing. The woman had such a tremendously large abdomen that she could not lie down in the cart. She had to kneel propping up her body on her two arms with great difficulty. She was very pale and there was little flesh on her bones, but she weighed 96 kilograms. A huge growth swelled her abdomen and filled half her chest cavity.

As soon as he saw the medical personnel, Zui clasped their hands saying 'I have brought to you for treatment a dying patient.'

The army medical personnel felt deep sympathy for their class sister. They knew that her condition was a consequence of the reactionary politics of China's enemies who had no concern for the sufferings of the working people. The PLA doctors decided they must cure her. But the equipment at their clinic was limited. What should they do?

They studied Chairman Mao's teaching: 'Weapons are an important factor in war, but not the decisive factor; it is people, not things, that are decisive.' They realised that the equipment they lacked could be made and they could learn the skills they needed.

"Dear Chairman Mao, it is you who have given me a second life."

At 7.30 am on 23 March all the members of the health section solemnly swore in front of Chairman Mao's portrait: 'We will follow your teaching "Heal the wounded, rescue the dying, practise revolutionary humanitarianism." We will do everything possible to remove this giant tumour and enable the patient to recover so that she can live and work happily in the great epoch of Mao Zedong.'

The operation lasted ten hours. The surgeons had to cope with many complications but in the end the operation was a success. After a few weeks the woman was working again in the commune fields. The success of the operation was thanks to the inspiration of Mao Zedong.

(from 'China Reconstructs', October 1968)

The terror of the Cultural Revolution

Mao Zedong's personality cult reached its height during the Cultural Revolution. During this chaotic period in China's history, attacks were launched on managers, experts, technicians and intellectuals. The attacks were brutal and humiliating as these sources show.

▶ *To what extent can Mao be held responsible for these terror attacks?*

SOURCE 2 — From a description of the scene at Amoy Middle School, 12 June 1966, given by a Red Guard, Ken Ling, who later left China for the West

On the athletic field, I saw rows of teachers, about 40 or 50 in all, with black ink poured all over their heads and faces. Hanging on their necks were placards with such words as "reactionary academic authority so and so", "class enemy so and so". . . They all wore dunce caps. . . Hanging from their necks were pails filled with rocks. I saw the principal, the pail round his neck was so heavy that the wire had cut deep into his neck and he was staggering. All were barefoot, hitting broken gongs as they walked around the field and begged Mao Zedong to "pardon their crimes". Beatings and tortures followed; eating night soil and insects; being subjected to electric shocks; forced to kneel on broken glass.

The many sides of Mao

One reason for Mao's great influence was that he had many careers. He was a peasant rebel, a military commander, a poet, a philosopher, a political leader.

▶ *In each of these roles he influenced China. What evidence can you find, in the source material on pages 84 to 89, to show Mao's influence through each of these roles?*

Role	Evidence
Peasant rebel	
Military Commander	
Poet	
Philosopher	
Political Leader	

SOURCE 3 — The memories of a six-year-old girl about the Cultural Revolution

Red Guards came to search our house, they confiscated everything. They took my father's books, my mother's jewellery, her college photo albums, everything. That was the end of my childhood. Our entire family was forced to move to a village eight hundred miles south of Beijing . . .

When we arrived, the local cadres took away the few things we had left, our clothes and our bedding. They left us only what we had on our backs. The family was put in the village schoolhouse, a small one-room building with holes in the wall where the windows should have been and a roof that leaked. There was no furniture. The peasants and cadres made my parents parade through the streets every day for several weeks. They hung a placard round my father's neck, they made him kneel down to confess his crimes and they beat both my father and mother with iron bars.

In that first year, our clothes soon became like tattered pieces of paper. I had to teach myself how to sew for the family by taking apart our old clothes and then putting them back together. We had to borrow or beg a few ounces of rice or sweet potatoes from the other peasants. Sometimes we were so short of food we had to eat the husks of the rice too. I would make them into pancakes. But they were so hard that I couldn't swallow them unless I was very hungry.

I want people outside China to know what the Cultural Revolution was like and what the Chinese have been through. I won't be happy till I die. I've never lived a good day in my life. My mother was beaten to death, my father was left senseless. That is what the Cultural Revolution did. It is unfixable. My scars will never heal.

(Fox Butterfield: 'China', 1982)

SOURCE 4 — Mao Zedong — assessing a legend

Mao Zedong was born in 1893 and he died in 1976. In that period almost everything in China seemed to turn upside down. An empire fell. Wars began and ended. Millions died. A new social system was established. The country of the wooden plough developed rocket technology. Mao lived through it all. He was the dominant figure of China in the twentieth century. He was one of the half-dozen or so most important rulers of the entire three thousand years of China's recorded history.

(adapted from 'Mao' by Ross Terrill, 1980)

Mao's Influence on China

Mao Zedong had a very significant impact on the history of China and dramatically affected the course of events in China this century. He influenced all aspects of life in China to one degree or another.

▶ *Discuss the extent of change in China. Was there a revolutionary change or very little change in these aspects of life in China under Mao? The class system – social organisation – the political system – political control – amount of freedom – worship of a leader – industrial production – agricultural production – position of women.*

Why did China change?

The answer to this question may seem obvious; that is, because the communists came to power in China. Things turned out as they did because China is a unique country with its own traditions, attitudes and heritage, and because the communists defeated the GMD in 1949 and put communist principles into practice. Yet it is not that simple; many things could have turned out differently.

There appear to be four main reasons for the way life developed under Mao Zedong:

1 Mao Zedong himself — his beliefs and policies and the direction he gave to the development of China.

2 Circumstances within China — such as: the severe weather conditions in the early 1960s which caused famine; the emergence of the Red Guard movement.

3 External Factors — such as: the outbreak of the Korean War; the withdrawal of Soviet aid.

4 The Chinese people themselves — the way in which they responded to the events which happened and the demands made on them.

▶ *What combination of reasons do you think led to the following:*
   a) the execution of landlords in the 1950s?
   b) the increase in steel production?
   c) the 100 Flowers Campaign?
   d) the terror of the Cultural Revolution?
   e) the hero worship of Mao?
   f) border clashes with the Soviet Union?

SOURCE 1 — A verdict

The story of Mao Zedong is the story of modern China. If Mao hadn't existed there would be no People's Republic of China today.

(from 'Mao for Beginners', Rius and friends, 1980)

▶ *This verdict on Mao's influence was written in 1980. Now that you've looked at the reasons for changes in China, do you agree?*

De-Maoification

Chinese offering a dollar a time for Mao

from Mary Louise O'Callaghan in Peking

THE CHINESE Government is trying to buy back the millions of Mao badges collected by Chinese during the Cultural Revolution. The badges, popular during the late 1960s when the Mao cult reached its height, are no longer sold openly in China.

But all Neighbourhood Committees — the lowest level of administration in China — have been ordered to pay up to $1 a badge in an effort to recall as many as possible.

The Chinese leadership, under Deng Xiaoping, has in recent years attempted gradually to dismantle the Mao cult, as the gap between Chinese policies and the late chairman's thoughts widens.

In 1981, a resolution was issued by the Chinese Communist Party declaring that Mao remained a "great revolutionary" despite his mistakes. But earlier this month the last remaining giant portrait of Mao on public display in Peking was removed from the front of the city's Imperial Palace.

However, the building is under renovation, in preparation for China's 35th National Day, and Chinese officials have declined to make clear whether the portrait will be returned to its place once the renovations are finished.

Late last year, the night spotlight on the portrait was mysteriously turned off, although officially the Chinese Government declined to acknowledge this.

The Guardian, March 28th 1984

Since Mao died there has been criticism of his style of leadership, and some have commented on the mistakes he made. Such criticism would have been unthinkable while he was alive. Some have called this process 'de-maoification'.

In recent years Mao's portrait has been removed from most public places. Another change is that radio news bulletins no longer start with a 'thought from the works of Mao', as they did when he was alive.

Below is one criticism of Mao.
▶ *How critical is Hua Guofeng?*
▶ *Why would he want to criticise Mao?*

SOURCE 2 — Chairman Hua blames Mao for mistakes

Beijing, 10 August — Chairman Hua Guofeng today openly blamed his predecessor, Mao Zedong, for 'serious mistakes made during the Cultural Revolution.'

Chairman Hua said he thought Mao, who died in 1976, was the most outstanding figure in Chinese history but added: 'He was a human being and not a god.'

Mr Hua's criticism, the most public yet made by a Chinese leader, came only a week after most of Mao's portraits were removed from public buildings in Beijing.

Chairman Hua said the events of the 30 years since the communists came to power in 1949, and especially the Cultural Revolution, would be investigated and discussed by the Twelfth Party Congress.

(adapted from 'The Guardian', 11 August 1980)

SOURCE 3 — Mad Mao lived as a recluse

Mao Zedong was virtually insane during the last 19 years of his life, according to the Chinese Communist Party general secretary, Zhao Ziyang. This statement was made at a dinner held after the recent Thirteenth Party Congress.

Zhao claims that from 1957 to 1976, when Mao died, the revolutionary leader 'had lost all touch with reality . . . and refused to emerge from the seclusion of his private residence' . . . 'Mao did not know or did not believe that peasants had starved to death in the terrible years after the so-called Great Leap.'

Until now many Chinese would have accepted that Mao was badly informed . . . But these claims will stagger them.

(Jonathan Mirsky, 'The Observer', December 1987)

Mao's portrait. Is the removal of Mao's picture from public places a sign of major political changes?

Understanding the Present, Preparing for the Future

To understand how and why things happen, we need to understand how things are caused and what motivates people. These cartoons illustrate some ideas about causation and motivation. Can you think of any examples from Chinese history that would illustrate them?

Why did they do it? What were their motives?

I WONDER WHAT THEY'VE COME FOR...?

Can we ever say that events are inevitable in history?

WORLD WAR III

THERE WAS NOTHING I COULD DO TO STOP IT

IS THERE ANYBODY LISTENING?

USSR

In history you study the past. Why? — because unless you understand the past you cannot understand the present. History also helps us to prepare for the future. It is impossible to predict the future exactly, but if you understand the past then there's a good chance you'll be prepared for future changes and events. For example:

► *Can you predict your life in five years' time? – Will you be married? Where will you live? Will you still be studying?*
► *Is it possible to predict your life in two years' time? – Will you still be at school? What job will you have? Who will you still be friendly with?*

You cannot be certain about the answers to these questions, but because you know your own past you will have some idea of what might happen to you in the future — all being well! Sometimes you can't anticipate what will happen, but you do know the kinds of things that would bring sudden changes — illness, moving to another part of the country, winning the pools.

Do historical events have one cause or several?

WHY DID YOU BUILD THE WALL HADRIAN?

I WANTED TO SECURE THE NORTHERN FRONTIER, TO KEEP PEOPLE BUSY, TO BE REMEMBERED FOR A GREAT CONSTRUCTION PROJECT.... BECAUSE I LIKE WALLS!

China — what might happen next?

In thinking about China an understanding of history helps us make sense of the present and prepare for the future. From studying its history, we know why China is communist; how people's lives have changed; why China is seeking the friendship of the West. However, we cannot predict the future of China; what we can do is see trends, patterns and likely developments.

So historians can suggest various possible ways in which events may develop. Historians can suggest what *may* happen and how China *may* change in the future.

► *Here are some of the various possibilities of what may happen in China. Examine each one. What evidence would support or contradict each possibility?*

1 As Western companies move into China it will be carved up as it was at the end of the nineteenth century.
2 The influence of the West will cause the Chinese to want more and more goods. This will bring about great inequalities in Chinese society and cause the collapse of communism.
3 The Chinese will want more freedom, as there is in the West, and will demand the end of strict communist control of their lives.
4 There will be a return to strict Maoist ways. There will probably be a new Cultural Revolution.
5 China is only using the West and getting what she can out of it. When she has got all she wants, China and the USSR will again become allies and turn on the USA and the West.

This cartoon was published after China was admitted to the UN in 1971. The USA had blocked China's entry since 1949. What did the cartoonist think was the reason for China's admission in 1971?

6 China will become the biggest manufacturing country in the world, begin fierce competition with the West, ruin our trade, and this will lead to war.

7 China will gradually develop into an advanced modern country and become a peaceful country, part communist, part capitalist.

8 China's large towns and ports in the east are the only parts benefiting from the new policies. The rural west is bitter at being left behind. In the end the country will split and there could be a civil war.

SOURCE 2 — What does the future hold?

Today the communist giants are no longer locked in sterile ideological combat but in a race to rationalise their economies — a race against each other as well as against the West. The prospect of a China 10 times the size of Japan, and with 10 times her productive capacity, will concentrate Mikhail Gorbachev's mind wonderfully. The powerful new incentive to modernise the Soviet economy itself should concentrate ours too. Will the two leading Marxist-Leninist countries compete with each other to introduce backdoor capitalism? Could all this hasten the start of the long retreat from communism? Strangely, does this vision offer us more threats than promises?

(from 'The Sunday Times', 5 May 1985, article by G. Walden, MP)

▶ What is meant by the last question in Mr Walden's article?

CHINESE SPELLING

A note on the spelling of Chinese names

There are two main ways of writing Chinese names using the English alphabet — the Wades-Giles system (Mao Tse-tung, Pekin) and the Pinyin system (Mao Zedong, Beijing). The Pinyin system is the new method and is used throughout this book as it supposedly produces pronunciation closer to the Chinese.

A 'c' in Pinyin is pronounced 'ts' and 'x' is 'sh' so try saying the name of the Empress Ci Xi with these sounds.

Here are listed some Chinese names in the Wades-Giles system and the Pinyin system as you may need to refer to some older books where the Wades-Giles system is used.

Wades-Giles	Pinyin
Kiangsi	Jiangxi
Shensi	Shaanxi
Yangtse-kiang (river)	Changjiang (river)
Yellow (river)	Huanghe
Pekin	Beijing
Canton	Guangzhou
Nanking	Nanjing
Sian	Xian
Yenan	Yanan
Kuomintang (KMT)	Guomindang (GMD)
Tz'u Hsi	Ci Xi
Teng Hsiao-p'ing	Deng Xiaoping
Chiang Ch'ing	Jiang Qing
Mao Tse-tung	Mao Zedong
Chiang Kai-shek } Sun Yat-sen }	remain the same

Index